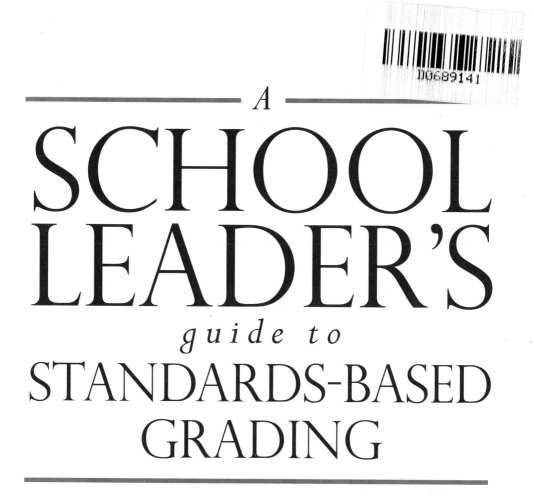

A SCHOOL LEADER'S *guide to* STANDARDS-BASED GRADING

TAMMY HEFLEBOWER, JAN K. HOEGH, & PHIL WARRICK

with Mitzi Hoback, Margaret McInteer, & Bev Clemens
foreword by Robert J. Marzano

MARZANO
—Research—

555 North Morton Street
Bloomington, IN 47404
888.849.0851
FAX: 866.801.1447
email: info@marzanoresearch.com
marzanoresearch.com

Printed in the United States of America

Library of Congress Control Number: 2014936131

ISBN: 978-0-9858902-8-5 (paperback)

18   17   16   15   8   9   10

Text and Cover Designer: Laura Kagemann

Marzano Research Development Team

Director of Publications
Julia A. Simms

Production Editor
Katie Rogers

Editorial Assistant / Staff Writer
Laurel Hecker

Marzano Research Associates

Tina Boogren
Bev Clemens
Jane Doty Fischer
Jeff Flygare
Tammy Heflebower
Mitzi Hoback
Jan K. Hoegh
Russell Jenson
Jessica Kanold-McIntyre
David Livingston
Pam Livingston

Sonny Magaña
Margaret McInteer
Diane E. Paynter
Debra J. Pickering
Kristin Poage
Salle Quackenboss
Ainsley B. Rose
Tom Roy
Gerry Varty
Phil Warrick
Kenneth C. Williams

Table of Contents

About the Authors

Tammy Heflebower, EdD, is a senior scholar at Marzano Research with experience working in urban, rural, and suburban districts throughout North America, Europe, Canada, and Australia. She has served as a classroom teacher, building-level leader, district leader, regional professional development director, and trainer. She was also an adjunct professor of curriculum, instruction, and assessment at several universities. Tammy received the District Distinguished Teacher Award and worked as an educational trainer for the National Resource and Training Center at Boys Town in Nebraska. She also served as director of curriculum, instruction, and assessment at Douglas County School District in Colorado and as a leader of many statewide organizations in Nebraska and Colorado. Tammy has coauthored several articles and the book *Teaching & Assessing 21st Century Skills* and is a contributor to *Becoming a Reflective Teacher*, *The Highly Engaged Classroom*, *Using Common Core Standards to Enhance Classroom Instruction and Assessment*, and *Coaching Classroom Instruction*. Tammy holds a bachelor of arts from Hastings College in Nebraska (where she was honored as an Outstanding Young Alumna), a master of arts from the University of Nebraska Omaha, and a doctorate of education in educational administration and an educational administrative endorsement from the University of Nebraska–Lincoln.

Jan K. Hoegh is an associate vice president of Marzano Research. She is a former classroom teacher, professional development specialist, assistant high school principal, and curriculum coordinator. Jan, who has twenty-eight years of experience in education, also served as assistant director of statewide assessment for the Nebraska Department of Education, where her primary focus was Nebraska State Accountability test development. She has served on numerous statewide and national standards and assessment committees and has presented at national conferences. An active member of several educational organizations, Jan was president of the Nebraska Association for Supervision and Curriculum Development. She is a member of the National Association for Supervision and Curriculum Development and Nebraska Council of School Administrators. Jan holds a bachelor of arts in elementary education and a master of arts in educational administration, both from the University of Nebraska at Kearney. She also earned a specialization in assessment from the University of Nebraska–Lincoln.

Phil Warrick, EdD, is an associate vice president of Marzano Research. He was an award-winning administrator for nearly twelve years, most recently as principal of Round Rock High School, which serves nearly three thousand students. Phil has been an adjunct professor at Peru State College since 2005. In 2010, he was invited to participate in the Texas Principals' Visioning Institute, where he worked with other principals to develop model practices for Texas schools. He is a past regional president for the Nebraska Council of School Administrators (NCSA). He also served on the NCSA legislative committee and was elected chair. In 2003, he was one of the first participants to attend the Nebraska Educational Leadership Institute, conducted by The Gallup Corporation at Gallup University in Omaha. Phil was named 1998 Nebraska Outstanding New Principal of the Year and Nebraska Secondary School Principals Region One Assistant Principal of the Year, 2004 Nebraska Secondary School Principals Region One Principal of the Year, and 2005 Nebraska State High School Principal of the Year. He earned a bachelor of science from Chadron State College and master's and doctoral degrees from the University of Nebraska–Lincoln.

Mitzi Hoback has been a professional development consultant and trainer for several years, working with teachers and principals in the areas of instruction, curriculum, assessment, and school improvement. She is former director of professional development for a regional education agency serving a five-county area in southeast Nebraska. With over thirty-five years as an educator, Mitzi has also been a classroom teacher at the elementary, middle, and high school levels; a lead teacher; and a coordinator of gifted education for a K–12 school district. Recognized as an educational leader who is student focused, Mitzi has presented at the state, regional, and national levels. She specializes in providing training in the implementation of effective instructional strategies, student engagement, vocabulary instruction, and quality assessment practices. She has facilitated data analysis, curriculum alignment, and the development of proficiency scales and high-quality formative and summative assessments with many school districts. Mitzi is a contributor to the book *Democratic School Accountability: A Model of School Improvement* and has served as the statewide chair of the Nebraska Educational Service Unit Professional Development Organization. She has received several awards, including the Nebraska Outstanding ESU Staff Member and Nebraska Association for the Gifted Extra Mile, and she was named to the Conestoga

Public Schools Hall of Fame. Mitzi holds a master of science in education with endorsements in assessment and gifted education from the University of Nebraska–Lincoln.

Margaret McInteer has worked in education for forty years. Throughout her career, she has developed positive, student-focused learning experiences. A dedicated and creative professional educator, Margaret has been successful in multiple roles in K–12 education. Most recently, she was a consultant in accreditation and school improvement at the Nebraska Department of Education. She worked with educators statewide, coordinating workshops and site visits, and also facilitated various state and district improvement processes and participated in planning initiatives. She began her career as a speech pathologist and later became director of special services in the Falls City, Nebraska, public school system, where she worked with financial planning and budgeting; parent and community involvement; individual educational plans; special education, Title I, and gifted program monitoring; and classroom management. As a professional development director for Educational Service Unit 4 in Auburn, Nebraska, Margaret created and delivered training to more than five thousand educators at regional, state, and national workshops over a span of eighteen years. She consulted with and provided technical assistance to districts on continuous school improvement, curriculum and assessment development, instructional strategies, classroom management, data retreats, and team building. Margaret has received numerous awards, including Jaycees Outstanding Young Educator, Outstanding Woman in the Community, Outstanding Educational Service Unit Staff Member, and the State of Nebraska Al Kilgore Award of Excellence for recognition of outstanding leadership in curriculum, instruction, and assessment. She earned a bachelor of arts and master of education in speech pathology and audiology from the University of Georgia.

Bev Clemens, PhD, is a curriculum coordinator for Douglas County School District, one of the largest school districts in Colorado. Bev leads teachers, principals, and administrators in the implementation of schoolwide and districtwide processes, initiatives, and reforms to improve instruction, curriculum, and assessment. An experienced classroom teacher, district leader, and professional developer, she has led the design and refinement of essential learnings, facilitated curriculum analyses to eliminate overlaps and gaps in student learning targets, and trained teachers and administrators in the development of high-quality formative and summative assessments. In addition, she has coordinated collaborative efforts to write proficiency scales, designed training to increase teacher content knowledge, researched the strengths and weaknesses of a district-based assessment system, and delivered training on high-quality instructional practices. Bev has served on numerous statewide standards and assessment committees and presented at national conferences. She understands the tremendous challenge schools and districts face in increasing student achievement, and she knows the pressure individual teachers are under as they work to implement practices to support students in their learning. This understanding, combined with her knowledge of curriculum, assessment, and instruction, creates a credible connection educators find compelling and inspiring. Bev offers practical ideas based on years of real experience and instills confidence and optimism in educators. Bev holds a bachelor of science degree in chemistry, and a master's degree and a doctoral degrees in science instruction and curriculum from the University of Colorado at Boulder.

Contributing Educators

Lisa D. Bucciarelli, EdD, serves as the assistant principal at Phoebe A. Hearst Elementary School in Chicago, Illinois. She has a doctorate of education in curricular studies from DePaul University, a master of arts in Spanish literature from Middlebury College, and an administrative license from Johns Hopkins University. Lisa has served as an educational leader for the past eighteen years. As a teacher leader and department chairperson, Lisa dedicated years to implementing effective world language pedagogy and best practice. Lisa is very active in the field of educational technology and is committed to the dissemination of knowledge regarding autism and diverse learning needs.

Robin J. Carey, PhD, is a director of educational programming and services for Douglas County School District in Colorado. She oversees programming for English learners and gifted learners and supports literacy interventions under the umbrella of response to intervention. She is president of the Colorado Association of Educational Specialists, a department of the Colorado Association of School Executives. Robin holds a bachelor of arts degree in music education from Concordia College in Moorhead, Minnesota, a master of arts in gifted education from the University of Northern Colorado, and a doctor of philosophy degree in educational leadership from the University of Denver.

Jeff Flygare has been a classroom teacher, professional developer, and English language arts content specialist for twenty-five years in Academy School District 20 in Colorado Springs, Colorado. Jeff helped lead his district's implementation of standards-based education, developed secondary standards-based curriculum (including an online English language arts curriculum), and served as coordinator of his school's gifted and talented programs. In 2010, Jeff received a Teacher Recognition Award from the U.S. Department of Education Presidential Scholars Program. He has been an active member of the National Council of Teachers of English throughout his career and was inducted into the Colorado Academy for Educators of the Gifted, Talented, and Creative in 1993. Jeff received his bachelor of arts degree in English from the State University of New York at Buffalo and holds two master of arts degrees in special (gifted) education from the University of Colorado at Colorado Springs and in English literature from the University of Colorado at Denver. Jeff is an associate for Marzano Research.

Mike Knoebel is originally from Algoma, Wisconsin, but studied middle school education at the University of Northern Colorado. He has twenty years of teaching experience in Colorado and has taught at Franklin Middle School in Greeley, Mesa Middle School in Castle Rock, and Rocky Heights Middle School in Highlands Ranch. His experience includes teaching math, science, social studies, health, and physical education. He is married to Kay, a nurse, and has two daughters, Mikayla and Delaney.

Missy Mayfield is the director of curriculum and learning management for Burkburnett Independent School District in North Texas. Missy has worked in curriculum and school improvement for over a decade, both with rural school districts and through a regional Education Service Center. She has a master's degree in gifted education and is currently finishing her doctoral degree in educational leadership.

Jennifer Murdock is a first-grade teacher at Buffalo Ridge Elementary in Castle Rock, Colorado. Born in Chicago, Illinois, and raised in Seattle, Washington, she has taught in special education, kindergarten, and first-grade classrooms for the past seventeen years. She earned a bachelor of arts degree in elementary education, an endorsement in P–3, and a master of education degree in technology in education. In her spare time, she enjoys playing soccer, skiing, hiking, and spending time with family and friends.

Kristin Poage is a classroom teacher in Bloomington, Indiana, and an adjunct faculty member at the Indiana University School of Education. She earned a bachelor of arts degree in English and history and a master of science degree in language education from Indiana University. She is currently working on her administrative leadership license. Kristin is very active in the area of grading and assessment and has served as a teacher leader in this area for her district through the creation of proficiency scales and the training and implementation of standards-based classrooms at all grade levels. She has also conducted a series of professional development webinars about moving from a traditional graded classroom to a standards-based classroom. Kristin is an associate for Marzano Research.

Cameron L. Rains is the curriculum and instruction specialist for Clark-Pleasant Community School Corporation in Indiana. Formerly, he was the director of elementary education for Monroe County Community School Corporation in Indiana. In addition to teaching third and fourth grades, Cameron has served as a literacy coach and a district instructional coach. He is passionate about ensuring that all students learn at high levels and has helped lead successful comprehensive assessment and grading reforms in two school districts.

Peter M. Richey, a former member of the United States Navy, is a middle school educator in the Chicago suburbs. He has taught seventh- and eighth-grade mathematics, social studies, and English and has served as a building-level leader. Peter is an avid believer in and proponent of standards-based grading, understanding that educational success is directly connected to students' understanding of learning targets. Peter earned his bachelor's degree in middle-level education from Illinois State University, his master's degree in curriculum from Northern Illinois University, and his master's degree in mathematics education from National Louis University.

Rex A. Sickmiller is a high school classroom teacher in Colorado Springs, Colorado. With his colleague, Michael Storrar, Rex has worked to implement standards-based instructional and grading practices in his classroom, school, and district. Rex's department has developed skills-based and standards-based curriculum maps that have been used throughout his district. Rex holds a master's degree in curriculum and instruction and serves as a faculty leader.

Linda Jo Stevens, EdM, is the director of curriculum and assessment in Lake Washington School District in Redmond, Washington. She has served as a classroom teacher, building-level leader, district administrator, consultant, and trainer in the areas of standards-based grading and proficiency. Linda began her career in Sweetwater County School District No. 1 in Rock Springs, Wyoming, where she received the district's Professional Excellence Award. She also served as a WYCET trainer in conjunction with the University of Wyoming. Later, Linda moved to Lake Washington School District, where she served as a teacher, professional developer, education association vice president, and district administrator. She also received the Golden Acorn Award for excellence in teaching. Linda holds degrees from Brigham Young University, the University of Wyoming, and City University of Seattle.

Michael Storrar is a classroom teacher in Colorado Springs, Colorado. Michael has spent the last seven years exploring and implementing standards-based grading. He led his math department in implementation efforts and assisted in spreading standards-based grading throughout his district. In addition to teaching at the high school level, Michael also serves as an adjunct professor of mathematics at Pikes Peak Community College.

Danielle S. Tormala, EdD, is the associate superintendent for the City of St. Charles School District in St. Charles, Missouri. She oversees student learning, curriculum, instruction, assessment, federal programs, principal supervision, comprehensive school improvement, and long-range planning. Danielle has also served as a classroom teacher, professional developer, assessment specialist, and administrator in several St. Louis–area school districts and has taught at the university level as an adjunct professor of curriculum, instruction, and assessment. She received her bachelor of arts degree from St. Louis University, a master of arts degree in educational leadership from Maryville University, and educational specialist and doctorate of education degrees in educational leadership from the University of Missouri–St. Louis.

Julie Williams has been the principal of Lincoln Elementary in the City of St. Charles School District in St. Charles, Missouri, since 2008. She graduated from the University of Iowa in 2000 with degrees in elementary education and mass communication and received a master's degree in school administration from Lindenwood University in 2002. She earned her educational specialist degree in educational administration from Lindenwood University in 2013.

About Marzano Research

Marzano Research is a joint venture between Solution Tree and Dr. Robert J. Marzano. Marzano Research combines Dr. Marzano's forty years of educational research with continuous action research in all major areas of schooling in order to provide effective and accessible instructional strategies, leadership strategies, and classroom assessment strategies that are always at the forefront of best practice. By providing such an all-inclusive research-into-practice resource center, Marzano Research provides teachers and principals the tools they need to effect profound and immediate improvement in student achievement.

Foreword

Grading is a well-entrenched element of education in the United States. As Lynn Olson (1995) observed, grades are "one of the most sacred traditions in American education. . . . The truth is that . . . grades have acquired an almost cult-like importance in American schools. They are the primary, shorthand tool for communicating to parents how children are faring" (p. 24). In 2004, grading expert Susan Brookhart noted, "In a perfect world there would be no need for the kind of grades we use in school today. . . . [But] grades are not going to disappear from schools anytime soon" (p. 4). This is certainly true; grades are here to stay.

However, acknowledging that grades are an important element of schooling does not mean that the current systems and processes used to assign grades are necessarily the most effective. Translating an entire body of information about students' performance and achievement over a quarter, trimester, or semester into one overall evaluation, or *omnibus grade*, is a daunting task for any teacher and not supported by much of the extant research. In 2007, John Hattie and Helen Timperley pointed out that "feedback is effective when it consists of information about progress, and/or about how to proceed" (p. 89). A single letter grade summarizing a student's performance in one content area does not provide this type of specific feedback. Additionally, teachers often consider nonacademic factors (such as attendance, participation, and behavior) when assigning grades, weight assessments or projects differently, and may misinterpret individual students' scores on exams or tests. Based on these factors and my experiences working with school leaders and teachers over the past four decades, I strongly advocate for a standards-based approach to grading (Marzano, 2000, 2006, 2010).

As Tammy Heflebower, Jan Hoegh, Phil Warrick, and their colleagues explain in the following pages, standards-based grading is a method of assigning grades that ties student achievement to specific topics within each subject area. It allows teachers, students, and parents to clearly communicate about specific areas of strength and need. Ultimately, standards-based grading gives a clear and concise answer to the student's question, What do I need to do to improve?

Despite the advantages of standards-based grading, which are described in detail in chapter 1, such an approach can be highly inaccurate if the leaders of a school do not implement systems that give teachers guidance and support regarding how to collect and interpret assessment data, assign grades, and translate those grades into specific scores for specific learning goals. Standards-based grading, when implemented effectively throughout a school or district, requires clearly delineated learning goals, proficiency scales to measure those learning goals, assessments to determine students' current status on each learning goal, and report cards that show exactly what students know. It requires teachers, students, and parents to reconsider long-held beliefs about what grades mean, how they should be assigned, and how they can be used appropriately. In the following pages, the authors walk school leaders through the process of implementing each element of an effective standards-based grading system, highlighting potential pitfalls, opportunities, and challenges.

Additionally, the authors have enlisted a large group of educators to contribute stories from their classrooms, schools, and districts about standards-based grading implementation. Readers are invited to step into these fine educators' shoes to experience firsthand the powerful results that standards-based grading can produce.

Although standards-based grading may seem like a substantial change to current grading and assessment practices, it is well worth the effort. A grading system that allows school leaders, teachers, students, and parents to improve student achievement over time, rather than simply reporting it at predetermined intervals, is an overdue change in many schools. I sincerely encourage readers to examine grading practices in their districts, schools, and classrooms and to take action to create systems and processes that provide accurate, consistent feedback to students about their current status and where they are headed next as they progress through school.

—Robert J. Marzano

Introduction

Standards-based education is centered on the idea that there are specific elements of knowledge and skill that all students should know and be able to do as a result of schooling. These essential elements of knowledge and skill are typically articulated in *standards statements*. Although standards-based education is common in the United States, it has often been adopted without commensurate changes to grading and reporting practices. This mismatch has led to confusion about how grades should be computed, what they mean, and how they should be used. An accurate and reliable process for grading students and reporting their progress is long past due in both policy and practice.

Our goals for this book are twofold: (1) to describe clear procedures, processes, and systems for implementing standards-based grading and reporting and (2) to present stories of educators and schools that have effectively implemented those procedures, processes, and systems. To address the first goal, each chapter describes an important aspect of standards-based grading (such as prioritized standards, proficiency scales, summative grades, report cards, exceptional students, and communication), addresses why it is important, and clearly and concisely explains how to implement it in a school or district.

To address our second goal, we have asked teachers, principals, curriculum directors, superintendents, and other educators across the United States to share stories of how they put these processes into practice in their classrooms, schools, and districts. We relay their challenges, successes, and lessons learned to help readers understand what the strategies we suggest look like in practice. John McKnight (1995) said, "In universities, people know through studies. In businesses and bureaucracies, people know by reports. In communities, people know by stories" (p. 171). This book is designed to synthesize research, articulate ideas, and share the stories of educators implementing various components of standards-based grading.

Overview of the Book

Standards-based grading "facilitates teaching and learning better than almost any other grading method" (Guskey, 2001, p. 26). Grading systems should ensure that students' grades are valid, fair, and consistent and clearly reflect what students know and are able to do. With those goals in focus, each chapter highlights a specific component of standards-based grading.

Chapter 1 details the differences between *standards-based* and *standards-referenced* grading and addresses why grading practices should change. Chapter 2 explains how to prioritize standards and create clear proficiency scales that articulate a continuum of performance levels for each standard. Chapter 3 explains how to design assessments based on proficiency scales that measure students' competence with each standard. In chapter 4, we provide guidelines teachers can use to determine a student's scores and grades. Chapter 5 addresses a special aspect of standards-based grading: grades for exceptional learners (students with special needs, English learners, and gifted and talented students). Finally, chapter 6 provides a big-picture view to guide school leaders and administrators as they design implementation plans for standards-based grading; communicate with students, parents, teachers, and community members about changes taking place; and guide their schools and districts through the transition to standards-based grading.

1

An Introduction to Standards-Based Grading

Grading is the primary means of reporting feedback about a student's level of learning. Robert Marzano (2010) described three types of grading: (1) norm-referenced grading, which involves comparing one student's performance to other students' performance; (2) self-referenced grading, which involves comparing a student's current performance to his or her past performance; and (3) standards-based grading, which involves assessing a student's competency with specific topics and standards within each subject area. In standards-based grading, students only begin to work on higher levels of knowledge and skill in a subject area once they have demonstrated competence, or proficiency, at lower levels. We agree with Susan Brookhart (2011) that standards-based grading is the most appropriate method of grading in a standards-based system and thus limit our discussion in this book to helping educators implement standards-based grading in their classrooms, schools, and districts.

Before we begin, however, we must clarify our terminology. Because the term *standards-based* is used more often than *standards-referenced* in educational conversations and publications about grading, educators often fail to make a distinction between the two systems. Nevertheless, there are critical differences.

Standards-Referenced Versus Standards-Based Grading

Grant Wiggins (1993, 1996) and Marzano (2010) described *standards-referenced grading* as a system in which teachers give students feedback about their proficiency on a set of defined standards and schools report students' levels of performance on the grade-level standards, but students are not moved forward (or backward) to a different set of standards based on their level of competence. Marzano (2010) observed, "The vast majority of schools and districts that claim to have standards-based systems in fact have standards-referenced systems" (pp. 18–19).

Standards-based grading is a system of assessing and reporting that describes student progress in relation to standards. In a standards-based system, a student can demonstrate mastery of a set of standards and move immediately to a more challenging set of standards. This means that if a third-grade student masters the entire set of third-grade mathematics standards in two months, that student immediately begins to work on fourth-grade mathematics standards. The same principle applies to all grade levels and subject areas: as soon as a student demonstrates competency with all of the standards for a specific level and subject area, he or she immediately begins working on the next level of standards for that subject area.

In order for students to move ahead to more difficult standards when they achieve proficiency with current standards (as in an authentic standards-based grading system), educators need to assign grades that clearly communicate students' current levels of performance for the standards they are working on. To achieve this type of feedback, grades must be based *solely* on students' current levels of performance with specific standards. Unfortunately, many grading practices currently used in the United States base grades on an assortment of additional factors beyond academic performance, such as a student's level of effort, innate aptitude, rule compliance, attendance, social behaviors, attitudes, or other nonachievement measures (Friedman & Frisbie, 2000; Ornstein, 1995). Including these measures in students' grades creates systems in which "grades are so imprecise that they are almost meaningless" (Marzano, 2000, p. 1). Genuine standards-based grading practices separate what students know and can do from how they behave and other nonachievement measures. Thus, while there are many ways that schools can improve student achievement, changing grading practices may be the most expedient way to address multiple issues at once.

Why Change Grading Practices?

Douglas Reeves (2008) stated, "If you wanted to make just one change that would immediately reduce student failure rates, then the most effective place to start would be challenging prevailing grading practices" (p. 85). The most effective grading practices provide accurate, specific, and timely feedback designed to improve student performance (Marzano, 2000, 2007; O'Connor, 2007). Rick Wormeli (2006) explained what a grade ought to be:

> A grade is supposed to provide an accurate, undiluted indicator of a student's mastery of learning standards. That's it. It is not meant to be a part of a reward, motivation, or behavioral contract system. If the grade is distorted by weaving in a student's personal behavior, character, and work habits, it cannot be used to successfully provide feedback, document progress, or inform our instructional decisions regarding that student—the three primary reasons we grade. (p. 19)

Unfortunately, many grades do not fit this description.

More than a third of all teachers believe that grades can serve as a meaningful punishment, despite extensive evidence showing this is not the case (Canady & Hotchkiss, 1989). David Conley (2000) found little relationship between the grade a teacher gave and whether or not a student was proficient. Multiple studies have shown that teachers who teach the same subject or course at the same grade level within the same school often consider drastically different criteria in assigning grades to students' performance (Cizek, Fitzgerald, & Rachor, 1995; McMillan, Myran, & Workman, 2002). Reeves (2008) stated:

> Three commonly used grading policies . . . are so ineffective they can be labeled as toxic. First is the use of zeroes for missing work. . . . Second is the practice of using the average of all scores throughout the semester. . . . Third is the use of the "semester killer"—the single project, test, lab, paper, or other assignment that will make or break students. (pp. 85–86)

These practices create inconsistencies in assigning grades that would likely never be tolerated in other venues, such as sports or medicine. Reeves (2008) added, "The same school leaders and community members who would be indignant if sports referees were inconsistent in their rulings continue to tolerate inconsistencies that have devastating effects on student achievement" (p. 86). Thomas Guskey (2011) compared the current practice of combining multiple measures into overall omnibus grades to combining unrelated health measures into a single score:

> If someone proposed combining measures of height, weight, diet, and exercise into a single number or mark to represent a person's physical condition, we would consider it laughable. How could the combination of such diverse measures yield anything meaningful? Yet every day, teachers combine aspects of students' achievement, attitude, responsibility, effort, and behavior into a single grade that's recorded on a report card—and no one questions it. (p. 19)

Andy Fleenor, Sarah Lamb, Jennifer Anton, Todd Stinson, and Tony Donen (2011) described grades as a game and explained that, sometimes, the best grades simply go to the students who do the most work:

> Quantity should not trump quality. Grades should be based on what students know and can do, rather than on how much work they can (and will) complete. Students should receive regular and specific feedback about what they know and don't know. Offering regular, specific feedback and grading that are based on learning and not behavior will have an immediate positive impact on your school. It will redefine students' role in the learning process, completely alter communication patterns with students and parents, and ultimately will improve performance top to bottom. (p. 52)

As Fleenor and his colleagues pointed out, resolving grading-system problems can have positive impacts throughout an educational system.

Grades should provide feedback to students, document their progress, and help teachers make decisions about what instruction a student needs next (Wormeli, 2006). When grades fulfill these goals, the effects on a school or district can be significant. Reeves (2011) found that effective grading policies reduced student failures, leading to

> a cascade of unexpected benefits: reduced discipline problems, increased college credits, more elective courses, improved teacher

> morale, fewer hours of board of education time diverted to suspensions and expulsions, and added revenues for the entire system based on a higher number of students continually enrolled in school. (p. 79)

Although changing grading systems can be challenging for school leaders and administrators, "the benefits are so great that it's worth doing" (Reeves, 2008, p. 87).

According to Grant Wiggins and Jay McTighe (2007), grading reform has been hindered by the idea that individual teachers should make their own decisions about how to teach:

> We believe teaching is currently far too personalized. Without long-term results and shared analysis of goals to study together or shared standards of best practice to which we refer, teachers have little choice but to (over)emphasize personal beliefs, habits, and style. Naturally, then, any criticism of our teaching makes most of us defensive and resistant to the message. (p. 111)

This overemphasis on personalization has resulted in grading systems that often defeat one of the main purposes of grades: feedback. Reeves (2006) stated,

> When it comes to providing students with feedback—and grading is one of many powerful sources of feedback—then I will argue that the freedom long enjoyed by private practitioners must take place within boundaries of fairness, mathematical accuracy, and effectiveness. (pp. 113–114)

Many teachers are forced to make their own decisions regarding grading because they do not receive any formal training on various grading methods, the advantages and shortcomings of each, or the effects of different grading policies on students (Brookhart & Nitko, 2008; Stiggins, 1991, 2008). Richard Lomax (1996) followed a group of elementary preservice teachers from just before their assessment course through the completion of student teaching. Although many issues were noted, grading proved to be the greatest source of difficulty for these teachers.

In many cases, the transition to standards-based grading requires educators, students, and parents to rethink and reframe beliefs about grading that they have held for many years. The process requires reflection, new learning, and changes in practice. Principals and administrators must also understand the research and theory behind standards-based grading. This large a transition requires a commitment to collegiality and collaboration, because improving grading systems and policies inherently involves improving schoolwide curriculum, instruction, and assessment practices. Essentially, standards-based grading is a high-leverage strategy that has the power to improve every other element of the system, which can be seen in the following accounts from a principal and several students.

Standards-Based Grading From a Principal's Perspective

To demonstrate the power of standards-based grading, we begin with the story of a building leader. Julie Williams is the principal of Lincoln Elementary in St. Charles,

Missouri, and her school's work with standards-based grading helped transform the school into a place where students are invested in their learning and work to achieve personal growth toward their goals. Julie explained that implementing standards-based grading meant helping students understand exactly what needed to be mastered at each grade level, where they were in the learning progression, and how they could work together to meet their goals. Even first graders are now able to explain what they are working on and how their learning activities will help them reach their goals. Students feel a sense of empowerment and work even harder since they are a part of the process. Although the percentage of students receiving free and reduced lunch has increased from 56.1 to 60.9 over the past four years, student achievement results have steadily improved. Figure 1.1 shows Lincoln Elementary students' average scores compared to district and state average scores on the Missouri Assessment of Progress (MAP).

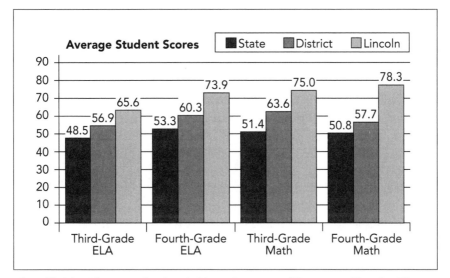

Source: Created by Julie Williams using data from the Missouri Department of Elementary and Secondary Education, 2013. Used with permission.

Figure: 1.1: 2012–2013 MAP results.

Julie said, "It has been an amazing journey, and there is no doubt that our work with standards-based grading has had a strong impact not only on our academic gains, but also on the culture of our school" (personal communication, August 29, 2013).

Standards-Based Grading From Students' Perspectives

To emphasize the importance of standards-based grading for students, we also present a few stories from students. The first is from Alex, a middle school student whose teacher, Kristin Poage, implemented standards-based grading at Jackson Creek Middle School in Bloomington, Indiana. Alex shared his perspective on the new grading and feedback system in a letter to his teacher:

Dear Ms. Poage,

When I earn a "3" on a paper that tells me that I have reached the goal and that I did everything right. I like knowing if I did it right and if I didn't get a "3" I know that I did something wrong. Plus the teachers' little notes also help me know that either I did a good job or got something wrong. They also help me know where I made the mistake and what I did wrong. I also know that I get a chance to redo something if I didn't do it right and that reassures me about my grade. Also, just having the standard on my paper tells me if I am performing to the standard of the assignment. When I get the paper back and it doesn't have a "3" I know that it isn't meeting the standards of the assignment and that I can do better. If I don't get a "3" I don't get down on myself, but instead I find out that I did something wrong and that I can redo it so that I meet the school and personal standard of the paper/assignment. I personally like having a number and a note. Like a "3" and a "Great job, keep it up" or a "2" and a "Good job on the grammar section, but the punctuation section needs some work. Let's work to redo it and turn it in tomorrow, I know you can do better!" That helps me a lot.

Alex

Source: Thomas Drew Frey. Used with permission.

Alex's letter highlights several of the benefits of standards-based grading. Rather than achieving an A and moving on, students are challenged to deeply understand content.

The next two stories are from high school students in Jeff Flygare's class at Air Academy High School in Colorado Springs, Colorado. Matt writes:

The standards-based grading system has had a profound impact on my development as a high school student. I view it as the only fair way to measure a student's academic performance in the classroom. All academic achievement should be measured by progress instead of an assiduous amount of tests and homework assignments. The progress that a student makes truly reflects all that is learned in the class. I first experienced the standards-based grading system during my sophomore year of high school. Like all of the other students and parents, I was rather skeptical at first. As the year began, I noticed my grades in the class were not all that desirable. At this point, I was even contemplating dropping out of the class. Luckily, I made a courageous decision to stick it out.

Eventually, I began to start getting better grades in the class. I noticed this transition around the middle of the semester. Finally, as the first semester ended, I had the grades that I desired. However, the standards-based grading system is intended to do much more than produce desirable grades. The real purpose of the system is to allow teachers and students to track each individual's learning progress throughout the year. So there I stood at the end of the first semester, with the grades I was hoping for, yet I was still curious about the true effects of standards-based grading. Since we tracked our grades on the four-point scale throughout the semester, I was able to find the assignments from the beginning and end of the semester. I found one essay that I wrote at the very beginning of the school year and an essay that I wrote at the very end of the semester. My writing had improved by an incredible amount. I noticed great advancement in my sentence structure, diction, analysis, and much more.

So then I asked myself this question, "Was it really possible for standards-based grading to produce such unbelievable results in such little time?" The simple answer is yes. The system has taught me to enhance my learning by focusing on specific topics within a broader subject. This is a very important process that most classes don't emphasize. In order to be a truly well rounded student, one must accentuate the areas that they excel at and focus on the areas that need improvement. By making clear cut goals and tracking the progress, the standards-based grading system maximizes any student's potential for academic success. Making clear cut goals also helps a student make sure that they have learned the necessary aspects of a class. The standards-based grading system has had a great impact on me as a high school student and I hope more students across the nation will be given the same opportunity I have had.

Source: John Najarian. Used with permission.

Madeline shared her perspective:

Standards based grading is a more human system of evaluation because it places more emphasis on the student in the classroom. Rather than being a hard average of points with set expectations, the standards based system allows for more exploration and learning because of its flexibility. The student is aware of exactly what is required for success, rather than being graded obscurely. This means that rather than measuring a student's ability to perform according to a specific system or subject, standards based grading is more likely to measure true learning.

Because of the clarity, simplicity, and adjustability of the standards based system, the student is more likely to succeed. The student is also more motivated, because unlike traditional grading, the standards based system is a positive reinforcement system. Rather than feeling defeated as the student watches grades decline over the course of the semester, the student will see improvement, feel less stress, and be more likely to enjoy and participate in learning.

The advantage to the student under the standards based grading system is that the student is empowered in the classroom. The student can take control of his or her grades, due to clearly defined goals and a healthier incentive to learn.

Source: Sophie Winkelmann. Used with permission.

As these communications exemplify, in a standards-based system, students take ownership for their learning and are intrinsically motivated to increase their knowledge and skill, rather than just collecting as many points as possible. These students' voices are reminders that students are the true consumers of education. As Neil Postman (1994) reminded us, "Children are the living messages we send to a time we will not see" (p. xi). Standards-based grading allows educators to teach students powerful lessons about taking responsibility for their own learning journeys.

Summary

Standards-based grading is an effective way to give feedback and evaluate students' performances using clearly defined criteria for specific learning standards. This clear communication gives students concrete guidance and useful feedback that they can use to improve their performance in specific areas. Although the shift from traditional grading practices to standards-based grading may require educators, students, and parents to reframe their existing beliefs and expectations about grades, the benefits to all stakeholders are powerful enough to warrant the change.

Prioritized Standards and Proficiency Scales

The first step in implementing standards-based grading is to clearly identify and articulate what students need to know and be able to do as a result of schooling. Those elements of knowledge and skill are usually articulated in standards. Often, however, there are more standards than can be taught in the instructional time available. Additionally, while standards usually articulate a target element of knowledge or skill, they do not always specify the simpler learning that students will need to acquire on their way to mastering the target. To address these issues, school leaders and administrators can help teacher teams prioritize standards and create proficiency scales.

Prioritized standards and proficiency scales clearly articulate what students should know and be able to do as a result of schooling. In many cases, individual teachers identify prioritized standards and create proficiency scales on their own to use in their classrooms. When teams of teachers use the same prioritized standards and proficiency scales, however, consistency from teacher to teacher and school to school increases. This consistency makes any differences in student achievement less dependent on which teacher a student is assigned and more reliably matched to the actual performance of that student on the criteria for a specific prioritized standard. Thus, we strongly recommend that administrators lead teams of teachers to collaboratively identify prioritized standards and create proficiency scales for those standards. Doing so requires input from teachers, of course. Here we present a process that leaders can use to identify teachers to participate in the process, help teachers prioritize standards, and help teachers write proficiency scales for the prioritized standards.

Identify Teachers

Prioritizing standards and creating proficiency scales requires content knowledge and teaching experience; thus it is essential for school leaders and administrators to create teams of teachers to complete this work. Ideally, this is a district committee. However, if a principal wanted to do this only at his or her site, it could be a school committee. Each grade level to which a given content area applies should be represented. For English language arts (ELA), this means involving K–12 teachers. For drama, this might mean involving teachers from grades 6–12. Obviously, including teachers at all grade levels is easiest if standards-based grading is being implemented across a district. If an individual school is implementing standards-based grading, we advise its leaders to collaborate with schools at other levels whenever possible to ensure a K–12 perspective.

Content-area teams for standard prioritization and proficiency scale work should be no larger than fifty people. The ideal is closer to forty, as it allows for strong representation from all stakeholders while maintaining a manageable group size to get the work done. Within these parameters, district and school leaders should strive to ensure the widest and fairest possible representation across their schools or district. In small districts, this team may include all staff members for the specified content area; in a large district, this team might include representatives from each school or feeder system. In a large high school, this may include only department chairs; if an elementary, middle, and high school are working together to complete this work, the group should include representatives from each grade level. Very small districts might join with neighboring districts or with their local intermediate education agency to ensure they have enough representatives from each grade level. A good rule of thumb when creating teams is to include at least three teachers per grade level or course, because the third teacher can function as a tiebreaker if the first two teachers disagree about what should or should not qualify as a prioritized standard.

Content-area teams should also include representatives from other important groups. Without exceeding fifty members, the team should include at least one special education teacher, at least one gifted education teacher, at least one administrator, and at least one teacher's union representative. It is important to help representatives from these groups learn about the process and clearly understand the nature of the work firsthand, as well as to enlist their help in distributing products and obtaining buy-in from teachers and schools. The following stories describe how two districts created teams for standards and scale work.

To create teams to work on prioritized standards and proficiency scales, Missy Mayfield, director of curriculum development and learning management in Burkburnett, Texas, identified a principal and assistant principal from each feeder system to participate. Those leaders then invited a math teacher, science teacher, social studies teacher, and ELA teacher from the middle or high school levels as well as a classroom teacher and specials (art, music, PE, foreign language) teacher from the elementary level. Each feeder system was also allowed to invite two or three extra members. Most feeders selected special education teachers or gifted and talented teachers to fill these spots.

As associate superintendent for the City of St. Charles School District in St. Charles, Missouri, Danielle Tormala's approach was slightly different. She decided to focus on individual schools (rather than the district system) as she recruited educators to prioritize standards and create proficiency scales. From each school, Danielle invited an administrator, an instructional coach, any grade-level teachers who volunteered to participate, the specials teachers, and the special education and English learner (EL) teachers. Whenever possible, Danielle included everyone who wanted to participate. Because this sometimes resulted in groups that were too big to do focused revision work on the standards and scales, Danielle recruited a smaller representative group to provide review and revisions from the work of the larger team.

To create teams like the ones described here, school and district leaders can use an application process or existing teams.

Application Process

Using an application process to select teachers for prioritizing standards and writing proficiency scales is an excellent option for a larger school or district where more than fifty individuals might want to participate in the process. An application process allows leaders to select teachers with the requisite knowledge and skills while also ensuring that all grade levels and groups are represented. Sample application questions for potential team members include the following:

- Briefly describe your content-area expertise (for example, advanced degrees or additional training in the content area).

- How would you determine which standards are most important (prioritized standards) for this content area?

- Please describe your experiences serving on other district or school teams.

- Why do you want to be a part of this content-area team?

- What grade levels do you teach?

- Which schools do you teach in?

- What else makes you a good candidate for this work?

Additionally, leaders should seek feedback from potential team members' principals and require each applicant's principal to sign the application so that principals are aware of the work teachers will be doing and understand how often teachers may be absent from their buildings. Leaders should then review candidates' applications and invite those who meet the specified criteria (grade-level representation, curriculum background, experience levels, mixed building representation, and knowledge of content and processes) to participate. This allows for the creation of a diverse and thoughtful group of teachers working toward a common, understood purpose. The following story explains how the application process worked in a Colorado school district.

Douglas County School District implemented an application process to select teachers for work with prioritized standards and proficiency scales. The Teacher on Special Assignment or coordinator for each content area at the district level created an application for his or her content area and invited teachers to apply through email. For example, the following email was sent to secondary science teachers:

Dear Teachers,

The Curriculum, Instruction, and Assessment Office is looking for teachers to be part of a team that will identify the most important learning targets for all students at each grade level (or for each course at the high school level). We anticipate the work will take two days of time; subs will be provided. Ideally, the study team will have representation from each secondary building and will include at least two teachers from each grade level. To apply, please complete the following application and return it to the Curriculum, Instruction, and Assessment Office by June 1st. (Note: Not all applicants will be accepted, since the study team needs to be balanced across schools, grades, and content expertise.)

Basic information:

- Name
- School where you currently teach
- Grades or courses you currently teach
- Grade or courses you have previously taught
- Total years of teaching experience

1. Why do you want to be a part of this work?

2. How do you decide what is most important to teach in your content area?

3. You and the other study team members may disagree about what is most important for students to learn. Please describe a situation in the past where you had a disagreement with a colleague. Explain how you worked through your disagreement.

4. Does your principal support your application to this study team?

Source: Curriculum & Instruction Team 2006–2007, Douglas County School District. Used with permission.

The questions were designed to give study team leaders pertinent information (demographics, applicants' awareness of current standards and trends in their content area, and so on), as well as make sure they had the right representation on the study team. Invitations were then issued to the selected teachers. A similar process was followed for study teams at the elementary level. Elementary teachers were asked to identify a first and second choice of grade level and content area to allow greater flexibility in filling out the study teams.

Additionally, district leaders checked with the local teachers' union to ensure representation. The teachers' union and district agreed to a 10 percent rule: if the teachers' union wanted to add additional teachers to a team, it could add up to 10 percent of the total group size. So, if there were forty people on the committee, the union could add up to four additional members.

Existing Teams

Instead of an application process, leaders might decide to use existing teams in their schools or districts. District teams that are already established, have a mix of grade-level representation, possess strong content knowledge and experience, and are accustomed to working together can often very efficiently prioritize standards and create proficiency scales. Examples of existing teams include curriculum councils, content committees, study teams, teams who have done work with standards and scales in the past, and professional learning community (PLC) collaborative teams.

When working with existing teams, it is important to remember four things: (1) more selling of the process and products may be necessary, since existing teams might feel strongly connected to previous work and see revision as unnecessary; (2) representation may not be as comprehensive and inclusive as with an application process; (3) the same group of people continuing to do all curriculum work means that information and expertise remains with the same representatives year after year; and (4) any existing collaboration conflicts may continue. However, each of these issues can be addressed. Honoring previous work and connecting it to the new work will help reduce ownership concerns. Adding team members in grade levels or content areas with existing gaps will ensure representation. Creating structures and processes for sharing information and seeking feedback can give a voice to individuals not on the committee, and adhering to group norms can help interpersonal conflicts. The following story illustrates how one district converted an existing team into one for prioritizing standards and writing proficiency scales.

Douglas County School District used existing curriculum councils to complete the prioritized standards and proficiency scales process for selected content areas. These councils were made up of representative teachers from each school, grade level, and content area who had served on a committee for materials selection for the district, who had been teaching their content for three or more years, and who already met during scheduled meeting times. By using existing teams for some content areas, the district was able to operate more efficiently and quickly. The refocus for the group was done by explicitly celebrating and connecting previous work to the new work. A letter was sent to each curriculum council member to honor their contributions and invite them to be a part of the newly revised structure.

> Dear curriculum council member,
>
> Your previous work has laid a solid foundation for the new work at hand. In order to continue to progress with our curriculum efforts in preparing students for their futures, we will make some changes to our existing curriculum council structure. Because of your previous commitment, we want to provide you with the first option to continue as a new study team member. Going forward, study teams will be more project oriented. For example, in past years, curriculum council members were on teams until they chose not to be. With our study team structure, we will meet with the team, complete the work, and disband the study team. This will allow for more teachers to be involved and contribute expertise for shorter amounts of time without committing to multiple years of service. New study teams will form when new curriculum, instruction, or assessment needs arise. This will allow more flexibility throughout our system.
>
> Sincerely,
>
> The Office of Curriculum and Instruction
>
> Source: Curriculum & Instruction Team 2006–2007, Douglas County School District. Used with permission.

The new structure and the idea that curriculum work now entailed more than just selecting materials were explained to teachers, who appreciated that the process honored the past yet provided new opportunities for involvement. The roles and responsibilities of those serving on the study teams were better understood by everyone involved, and school leaders encouraged teachers' involvement in curriculum efforts at the school level.

Once teams are in place, school leaders must guide them through the process of prioritizing standards.

Prioritize Standards

When it is not possible to teach all that the standards designate in the time available, some standards need to be emphasized over others. Although these emphasized standards have been called by other names (for example, *power standards*; Reeves, as cited by Ainsworth, 2003), we prefer the term *prioritized standards* (Ainsworth, 2003). Prioritized standards are those that have been identified as most essential to a particular grade level, content area, or course. Although it is still important to teach standards that are not deemed prioritized, teachers devote significant time and resources to ensuring that prioritized standards are mastered. For example, if thirty standards are listed in the Common Core State Standards (CCSS) for a grade level or course, a teacher might prioritize fifteen of those and teach the remaining fifteen as subcomponents of the prioritized ones. Alternatively, the teacher might teach standards that aren't prioritized independently but spend less time on them. Ideally, decisions about which standards are prioritized will be made collaboratively by teacher teams at the school or district level.

Because different sets of standards may be used for different content areas (for example, the Common Core for ELA and mathematics, the Next Generation Science Standards [NGSS] for science, and individual state standards for social studies and history, the arts, and other subjects), it is important to review all sets of prioritized standards to ensure that they specifically and clearly articulate exactly what students are expected to know and be able to do. Ideally, standard prioritization and proficiency scale creation is done one content area at a time. Although scales should ultimately be written for all content areas, we recommend beginning with mathematics since it is quite linear in nature, which will provide momentum for the process and give educators valuable experience. Once teachers and leaders are familiar with the process, the remaining content areas can be addressed.

Prioritized standards can include both declarative and procedural knowledge, and understanding the difference between the two is an important aspect of creating proficiency scales for them. *Declarative knowledge* is informational and is often signaled by the word *understand*. For example, a declarative standard says, "Students will understand the key concepts of molecular bonds." *Procedural knowledge* includes skills, strategies, and processes (Anderson & Krathwohl, 2001; Marzano & Kendall, 2007) and may be signaled by words and phrases such as *demonstrate* or *be able to*. For example, a procedural standard says, "Students will demonstrate how a covalent bond forms." Sometimes a standard asks students to combine knowledge and processes. For example, "Students will use their knowledge of molecular bonds to explain the difference between covalent and noncovalent bonds, demonstrating if necessary." Depending on the standards, it is likely that sets of prioritized standards will contain a combination of procedural and declarative knowledge.

In addition to prioritizing standards, educators may also need to ensure that the standards are phrased in ways that clearly reflect what students need to know and be able to do. Awkward or vague phrasing can hinder educators from agreeing on what the standard means and can prevent students from clearly understanding what is expected from them. For example, "read for meaning" is less specific than "read for specific ideas, information, and ideas shared by the author." Marzano (2009) said:

> The research strongly implies that the more specific the goals are, the better they are. That is, goals that are specific in nature are more strongly related to student achievement than goals that are not. . . . Specific goals provide a clear direction for behavior and a clear indication of desired performance, and as such they serve as motivators. (pp. 4, 6)

Edwin Locke and Gary Latham (1990) found that having specific goals was associated with effect sizes ranging from 0.42 to 0.80, which translates to a percentile gain of 16–29 points. That is, students who normally score in the 50th percentile would be expected to score in the 66th–79th percentile when provided with clear and specific goals. By unpacking standards, educators are able to create clear, specific goals.

To begin the prioritization process, leaders first help teachers by explaining criteria that should be considered when evaluating standards to decide if they should be prioritized or not. Second, leaders allocate time and space for the work to happen. Finally, leaders use a four-step process to help teachers navigate the actual prioritization of the standards.

Criteria for Prioritized Standards

Before teams begin to identify prioritized standards, they must understand the criteria for determining which standards should be prioritized. According to Larry Ainsworth (2003), there are three criteria to consider when determining which standards to prioritize:

1. **Endurance**—Knowledge and skills that will last beyond a class period or course

2. **Leverage**—Knowledge and skills that cross over into many domains of learning

3. **Readiness**—Knowledge and skills important to subsequent content or courses

Our experience has indicated that two additional criteria should also be considered:

4. **Teacher judgment**—Knowledge of content area and ability to identify more- and less-important content

5. **Assessment**—Student opportunity to learn content that will be assessed

As an example of how teachers can evaluate a specific standard for these five criteria, consider the following ELA standard from the CCSS:

> Interpret information presented visually, orally, or quantitatively (e.g., in charts, graphs, diagrams, time lines, animations, or interactive elements on Web pages) and explain how the information contributes to an understanding of the text in which it appears. (RI.4.7; National Governors Association Center for Best Practices & Council of Chief State School Officers [NGA & CCSSO], 2010a, p. 14)

This standard demonstrates endurance, leverage, and readiness—students will use these skills long after the test, in multiple disciplines, and in other content areas or courses. It also has strong teacher judgment and assessment connections. In contrast, consider a Common Core standard related to speaking and listening:

> Add audio recordings and visual displays to presentations when appropriate to enhance the development of main ideas or themes. (SL.4.5; NGA & CCSSO, 2010a, p. 24)

While this standard may have some measure of endurance and leverage, it contains fewer readiness skills than the first standard. When asked to use their judgment, many teachers indicate that SL.4.5 should be a subordinate standard that is connected to and taught in concert with more important speaking and listening standards. Finally, audio recordings and presentations may not connect as directly to a district or state assessment as the types of texts listed in RI.4.7 do. Therefore, an ELA teacher team might decide to make RI.4.7 a prioritized standard but not SL.4.5.

A matrix like the one in table 2.1 can assist in the process of identifying prioritized standards according to these criteria.

Table 2.1: Prioritized Standards Decision Matrix

Standards	Endurance	Leverage	Readiness	Teacher Judgment	Assessment
RI.4.7: Interpret information presented visually, orally, or quantitatively (e.g., in charts, graphs, diagrams, time lines, animations, or interactive elements on Web pages) and explain how the information contributes to an understanding of the text in which it appears. (NGA & CCSSO, 2010a, p. 14)	X	X	X	X	X
RL.4.7: Make connections between the text of a story or drama and a visual or oral presentation of the text, identifying where each version reflects specific descriptions and directions in the text. (NGA & CCSSO, 2010a, p. 12)	X	X			
SL.4.5: Add audio recordings and visual displays to presentations when appropriate to enhance the development of main ideas or themes. (NGA & CCSSO, 2010a, p. 24)	X	X			

As seen in the table, RI.4.7 meets all of the criteria, but the two subsequent standards (RL.4.7 and SL.4.5) meet only two criteria each. This is not to imply that these standards are not important or should not be taught. They must be taught. However, there may not be a dedicated assessment for these skills. Instead, they might be assessed in the context of another skill. Most likely, teachers will also spend less instructional time on them compared to prioritized standards like RI.4.7.

Time and Space

Although time and space may seem like prosaic concerns, ensuring that teachers have time for important conversations and space with the appropriate materials for their work is extremely important to the successful completion of prioritized standards and proficiency scale work. Paying attention to these small details communicates to teachers that their work is important and prevents small problems or time constraints from hindering efforts.

For each content area (mathematics, ELA, social studies, science, and so on), it is best to have one full day (five to six hours) of concentrated team time to identify prioritized standards. However, if a district or school wants to identify prioritized standards in several content areas simultaneously, it could compress the amount of time needed by doing large-group training about the process with several teams together (for example, the math team, the ELA team, and the science team combined) and then splitting them into content teams for the rest of the work. In this way, three content areas could be finished in about twelve hours rather than the expected fifteen to eighteen.

As stated previously, it is best if work in each content area can be finished in one contiguous session. However, we recognize that this is not always possible. If contiguous time is not available, leaders can use existing meeting times, such as PLC meetings, after-school meetings, monthly curriculum meetings, or professional development meetings. When using a series of short meetings, it is important to keep in mind that the work may take longer. For example, identifying prioritized standards during a series of one-hour meetings will probably take seven to eight meetings rather than the equivalent five to six contiguous hours.

Whichever meeting structure is used, leaders can facilitate the work by providing appropriate space and materials for each team. It is best if each grade-level group has a space in which to collaborate (for example, a round table). Each grade-level group should also have access to the following supplies:

- A copy of existing state standards documents for the content area of focus
- Highlighters
- Sticky notes
- Chart paper and markers

In addition, each member of each group should have a copy of the standards and a place to take notes.

Prioritization Process

The basic four-step approach to prioritizing standards is to (1) analyze standards documents to identify important content, (2) select preliminary prioritized standards and write them on sticky notes, (3) categorize the prioritized-standard sticky notes by strand and theme, and (4) review the final categories for gaps or missing knowledge and skills. These four steps provide an outline that school leaders can use to explain the process to teachers and monitor teams' progress.

While the basic process works well in most situations, individual groups and teams may have unique needs to which school leaders should be sensitive. For example, teams may have worked on similar prioritization projects in the past, or specific teams might consist of extremely experienced content experts. Table 2.2 summarizes considerations that may prompt leaders to differentiate the basic process for teams' unique needs.

Table 2.2: Differentiating the Prioritized Standards Process

Use the basic process if . . .	Differentiate to value previous work if . . .	Differentiate to value teacher experience and content expertise if . . .
You have less-experienced teachers on the team, or you have a very tight timeline.	Your school or district has identified prioritized standards in the past but needs to align them to new standards (such as the CCSS or NGSS).	You have very experienced staff members on the team.
You are not as concerned about drawing out the content expertise of your teachers. You simply want to get the work completed.	Your staff is already very familiar with your state's standards documents.	Teachers have done curriculum work before and are content experts.
You have few, if any, meeting structures in place. You may have to get this done during a limited number of workdays.	You have structures and processes already in place for engaging in collaborative work.	You have structures and processes already in place for engaging in collaborative work.
You don't have a teachers' union, or your union is typically supportive of your efforts around curriculum.	You have an involved teachers' union, and it is amenable to the alignment work that is necessary.	You have a strong teachers' union and must often defend curriculum work and get buy-in for structures and processes.

As seen in the second column of table 2.2, a team could be composed of teachers who have already done similar work in the past or are in a district or school in which similar work may have already been done by other teams, as is the case in some U.S. states (for example, New York, Washington, Iowa, and Arkansas). If that is the case, the administrator will want to honor previous work and ensure that he or she is not asking teachers to redo work unnecessarily. Additionally, identifying previous efforts that are still useful (or only require light revision) will save time and effort.

A team could also be composed of teachers with significant experience and content knowledge, as shown in the third column of table 2.2. If that is the case, leaders will want to value teachers' background knowledge and experience. This usually involves eliciting teacher perspectives first about what standards should be prioritized and then comparing teachers' judgments with standards documents.

Here, we explain each step of the basic process and provide differentiation strategies for the unique needs of various groups.

Step 1: Analyze Standards Documents

Prior to the team's first meeting, distribute copies of applicable content-area state standards documents to the teachers on the team and request that they read through the documents and become familiar with the content *before coming to the first meeting*. If it is impossible for teachers to complete this work beforehand, allow about an hour for teachers to read the documents at the first meeting. This step *must* be completed by all groups of teachers, regardless of previous prioritization work or teachers' levels of experience. However, when working with highly experienced teachers, postpone this step until after step 2. If teachers are already very familiar with the standards documents, allocate a shorter amount of time for reading them. All teachers involved in the process must have a firm understanding of the current standards documents, and reading through them is the only way for team members to gain that understanding.

Step 2: Select Preliminary Prioritized Standards

After reading the standards documents, teachers independently identify three levels of content in the documents: (1) content that is important for students to know, (2) content that is helpful for students to know, and (3) supplementary content. Important content should be highlighted in pink, helpful content should be highlighted in yellow, and supplementary content should be highlighted in green. The colors are analogous to a stoplight: Pink means "Stop! Pay close attention. This is important." Yellow means "Caution—likely important." Green signifies "Go! It may be possible to let this go." Limit the time spent on this task to thirty to forty minutes. This will keep teachers from deliberating too long over any one standard; the goal is to get a gut reaction about the importance of each standard. Remind teachers that their first impression is probably the most reliable at this stage.

After they complete their individual ratings, teachers form grade-level or course-specific groups. Teachers compare their ratings with others' in their group and explain their decisions. Then the team considers the criteria of endurance, leverage, readiness, teacher judgment, and assessments using the checklist from table 2.1 (page 19). This allows the teachers to check their initial judgments against the criteria and examine their thinking. The goal is for each group to reach a general consensus about which standards should be prioritized for its grade level or course. This step takes approximately one to two hours.

If previous standard prioritization work has been done and the goal is to align previous prioritized standards to new standards documents (such as the CCSS or NGSS), use the highlighting procedure to identify various levels of alignment (rather than importance) between existing prioritized standards and the new standards. Highlight strong existing alignment (same content at the same grade level) between existing prioritized standards and new standards with green (to represent *go*). Identify content that is present in both documents but at a different grade level or in a different course with yellow (to represent *caution*), and identify content represented in the new standards but not in existing standards with pink (to represent *stop*). Notice that this coding system is slightly different from that described previously; it is designed to guide next steps by emphasizing the pink and yellow sections. Green standards are left alone, as they represent good alignment between the new standards and the previous prioritized standards. Yellow standards are moved to the grade level at which they appear in the new standards documents, since students will ultimately be assessed at the new grade level. Pink standards are then evaluated according to the criteria for identifying prioritized standards. Those added to the existing prioritized standards should be added at the grade level they appear in within the new standards. As in the basic process, the end goal is for grade-level teams to reach consensus about which standards should be prioritized for each grade level.

If your team consists of highly experienced teachers, have them use their professional judgment to independently list important content for students to learn at their grade level or in their courses *before* they look at any standards documents. Next, have them discuss their lists with other grade-level or course teammates, explaining what they listed and why. Here, the goal is for teachers to agree on which standards should be most important at their grade level *before* they look at any standards documents. Then, distribute copies of the standards documents to each teacher for his or her grade level or course and give teachers time to read the documents. Ask teachers to compare their lists of important content to the standards documents and fill in any important content or information that they initially failed to list. They should also cross out information in their lists that does not appear in the standards documents. Again, the goal is for each grade-level team to agree on which standards should be prioritized.

Teachers should also address the amount of time necessary to teach all of the standards noted for each grade level. Each group should discuss and denote the number of days (one class period equals one day) that will be required to teach each prioritized standard to mastery. Noting this time next to each standard will help the team further prioritize the standards. Those that take more time to develop conceptual understanding will likely be a higher priority. Teams should consider whether any standards can be combined and which standards should be less emphasized according to the criteria previously discussed (endurance, leverage, readiness, teacher judgment, and assessment). Revisiting these criteria during revision can help teams further clarify and refine their original decisions.

Step 3: Categorize Prioritized Standards

Steps 3 and 4 are always used sequentially regardless of whether previous work has been completed or teachers are experienced. After the prioritized standards have been identified and agreed on by each grade level or course group, teachers write each standard on a separate sticky note. This should only take about fifteen to thirty minutes. To save

time, teachers can cut apart the criteria charts (see table 2.1, page 19) where they identified the prioritized standards and add tape to the slips with the prioritized standards
(creating a preprinted sticky note). Once each prioritized standard has been written on a
sticky note, teams group the standards into common themes by arranging the sticky notes
into an affinity diagram (Charantimath, 2006), which groups similar items according to
categories, as shown in figure 2.1.

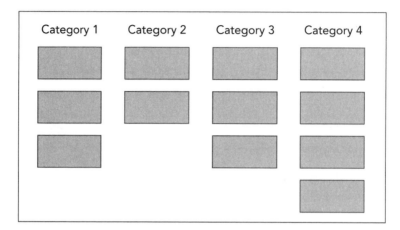

Figure 2.1: Affinity diagram for prioritized standards.

A group prioritizing standards in ELA might organize its standards within the CCSS
strands. A group working in mathematics might organize the standards into the CCSS
domains. This part of the process usually takes fifteen to twenty minutes. Once the prioritized standards have been categorized, teams should list the categories and prioritized
standards on separate pieces of chart paper, printing the grade level or course at the top
of each chart page.

Step 4: Review the Final Categories

Begin step 4 by displaying the charts of prioritized standards from step 3 around the
room. Use a rotating review strategy (Kagan & Kagan, 2009) to give teams the chance to
review other grade-level or course-specific groups' lists (particularly at grade levels above
and below or for courses taken before or after their own). Each team leaves one person
(called the chart leader) from the team at its own chart to explain which standards were
identified as prioritized standards and why. The other team members rotate to review the
other charts. Every three to five minutes, the administrator or leader prompts groups to
rotate to a new chart, prompts the chart leader at each chart to explain his or her group's
decisions and rationale, and prompts groups at each chart to ask questions of and offer
suggestions to the chart leader (which he or she records). This strategy allows teachers to
see how the prioritized standards fit together and where key concepts may require further
separation or inclusion.

As mentioned previously, it is especially important that grade-level teams review the
grade levels above and below their own. Leaders can decide whether or not to have the

teams rotate to every chart or just those adjacent to their own grade levels. Upon completion of the rotating review, each team returns to its own chart to review and revise its work based on comments received. Teams should track each accepted and incorporated revision as well as revisions that were declined by the group, along with the rationale for accepting or declining the revision. These notes can become the basis for a frequently asked questions (FAQ) document. This part of the process takes approximately one hour.

Ideally, the process described here will be used by teams of teachers. However, individual teachers can also use the process to identify prioritized standards on their own. In the following story, Jeff Flygare, an ELA teacher in Colorado Springs, Colorado, used this four-step process to identify prioritized standards as a pilot project before his whole school began the work.

Jeff had been teaching Advanced Placement (AP) English Literature and Composition for the better part of two decades, and he felt like he knew what his students needed to know to do well on the AP test. Yet every year, a few of his students did not do well. He wanted to find a way to ensure that everyone was successful, so he turned to the College Board course description for AP English Literature and Composition (standards document) for help. There, he found descriptions of the kind of work students should be able to do to perform well on the AP test. Before reading through all the descriptions, he brainstormed a list of the information and skills he already taught in class. Then he compared his brainstormed list with the knowledge and skills from the course description and used specific criteria to identify the standards that were most important. He classified them into categories and estimated how long it would take to teach each one. Based on the prioritized standards he identified, he revamped the content for all five classes he was going to teach that year—three senior AP English Literature classes and two junior AP English Language classes.

In order to use prioritized standards to create proficiency scales, the lists of prioritized standards will need to be typed and saved as electronic documents. Leaders can arrange for this to be done outside of group work time or can ask teachers to type and save their final lists of prioritized standards at the end of step 4. If all of the teachers in a district or school have access to a shared drive on a network, we suggest that leaders create a folder for each content area on that shared drive. Within each content-area folder, there should be separate folders for each grade level. All prioritized standards lists should be saved in the appropriate folders. If a district or school does not have a shared drive or network, all electronic lists of prioritized standards should be emailed to one individual responsible for organizing and archiving the files.

Write Proficiency Scales

Once teams have prioritized and clearly stated the standards, they must create proficiency scales for them. Proficiency scales articulate learning progressions for each prioritized standard. Learning progressions describe how students' understanding of a topic develops over time (Daro, Mosher, & Corcoran, 2011; Heritage, 2008). Table 2.3 shows a generic proficiency scale.

Table 2.3: Generic Proficiency Scale

Score 4.0	In addition to score 3.0 performance, the student demonstrates in-depth inferences and applications that go beyond what was taught.	
	Score 3.5	In addition to score 3.0 performance, partial success at score 4.0 content
Score 3.0	Target goal	
	Score 2.5	No major errors or omissions regarding score 2.0 content and partial success at score 3.0 content
Score 2.0	Simpler goal	
	Score 1.5	Partial success at score 2.0 content and major errors or omissions regarding score 3.0 content
Score 1.0	With help, partial success at score 2.0 content and score 3.0 content	
	Score 0.5	With help, partial success at score 2.0 content but not at score 3.0 content
Score 0.0	Even with help, no success	

Source: Adapted from Marzano, 2010.

As seen in table 2.3, only two levels change from scale to scale: scores 3.0 (the target goal) and 2.0 (the simpler goal). Score 3.0 is simply the prioritized standard, while score 2.0 consists of simpler knowledge and skills that students will need to acquire before they can demonstrate proficiency for the target goal. (It is important to note that some teachers, schools, and districts prefer that the score 4.0 level also be explicitly stated.)

Score 4.0 indicates that a student has demonstrated learning, inferences, and in-depth understanding that go beyond the target goal; score 1.0 indicates that with help from the teacher, the student is able to demonstrate partial knowledge of the 2.0 and 3.0 content; and score 0.0 indicates that even with help, a student is unable to demonstrate success with any of the content. The half-point scores allow teachers to assign scores at a finer level of detail than can be done with whole-point scores alone. For example, if a student knows and understands the 2.0 content, but has only partial success with the 3.0 content, that student would receive a score of 2.5. Likewise, if a student knows the target 3.0 content and has partial success with the 4.0 content, he or she would receive a score of 3.5.

As an example of how a proficiency scale is created for a specific prioritized standard, consider the following sample life science standard:

> Students will develop and use a model to illustrate the hierarchical organization of interacting systems that provide specific functions within multicellular organisms. (Douglas County School District, 2007)

The prioritized standard is inserted into the 3.0 level of the scale, and simpler knowledge and skills are articulated in the 2.0 level of the scale, as shown in table 2.4.

Table 2.4: Proficiency Scale for Life Science

Life Science: Structure and Function		
4.0	In addition to score 3.0 performance, the student demonstrates in-depth inferences and applications that go beyond what was taught.	
	3.5	*In addition to score 3.0 performance, partial success at score 4.0 content*
3.0	The student will develop and use a model to illustrate the hierarchical organization of interacting systems that provide specific functions within multicellular organisms.	
	2.5	*No major errors or omissions regarding score 2.0 content and partial success at score 3.0 content*
2.0	The student will: • Know vocabulary such as *organisms, organ systems, organs, tissues, cells,* and *life processes* • Explain that all living things are made of cells (one or many) • Describe the function of a cell and how the parts of the cell contribute to the function of the cell as a whole • Explain that the body of an organism is a system made of up subsystems (all made of cells) that perform life processes • Explain that sensory receptors respond to stimuli by sending messages to the brain for immediate behavior (for example, move away) or storage (for example, as a memory)	
	1.5	*Partial success at score 2.0 content and major errors or omissions regarding score 3.0 content*
1.0	With help, partial success at score 2.0 content and score 3.0 content	
	0.5	*With help, partial success at score 2.0 content but not at score 3.0 content*
0.0	Even with help, no success	

Source: Douglas County School District, 2007.

As seen in table 2.4, simpler knowledge and skills at the score 2.0 level often involve understanding vocabulary related to the target goal, explaining knowledge that is foundational to the target goal, or performing parts of processes that are necessary to achieve the target goal.

In order to bring prioritized standards to life in the classroom, proficiency scales must be written for them. As explained previously, proficiency scales clearly describe what students need to know and be able to do at varying levels of performance for each prioritized standard. Like identifying prioritized standards, creating proficiency scales is best done in teams. If possible, the same teams that identified the prioritized standards should create proficiency scales, as they will already have a solid understanding of the content and skills in the prioritized standards. However, substituting a few new team members as needed may decrease the workload on each teammate and allow more teachers to participate in the process.

Before teams begin work, they should examine existing proficiency scales to see if they can use or modify those scales to align with the prioritized standards. Over 1,800 proficiency scales for various content areas and grade levels are available at **itembank .marzanoresearch.com**. Using preexisting scales as a base is particularly helpful in grade levels or content areas with only one or two teachers. The scales in the database are searchable by topic and grade level. Additionally, there are proficiency scales for all standards in the CCSS. Although these scales can be very helpful as reference points, it is important to modify them for the unique needs of your school or district.

Draft Proficiency Scales

The most efficient way to draft proficiency scales is to divide and conquer: teams decide which member will work on scales for each of the prioritized standards and then review one another's work together once the scales have been drafted. It is important, however, to have each team of teachers create one full proficiency scale together before working individually so that every member of the team clearly understands each level of the scale and how to draft it.

Teachers begin by selecting a prioritized standard. For example, consider CCSS RI.4.7, which teachers in a previous example identified as a prioritized standard:

> Interpret information presented visually, orally, or quantitatively (e.g., in charts, graphs, diagrams, time lines, animations, or interactive elements on Web pages) and explain how the information contributes to an understanding of the text in which it appears. (RI.4.7; NGA & CCSSO, 2010a, p. 14)

The prioritized standard is listed next to score 3.0 on the proficiency scale. Then, teachers identify the simpler knowledge and skills required to master the prioritized standard. For RI.4.7, simpler content might include:

- Recognize and recall specific vocabulary such as *information, visual, oral, quantitative, chart, graph, time line, animation, interactive, webpage*, and *text*.

- Identify patterns in information presented visually, orally, or quantitatively (such as sequence, comparison, and cause and effect).

- Recognize connections between figures and tables in a text and the text itself.

These simpler knowledge and skills are listed next to score 2.0 on the proficiency scale. Teachers do not fill in content for the 4.0, 3.5, 2.5, 1.5, 1.0, 0.5, and 0.0 levels on the proficiency scale, instead leaving the generic statements in those sections. The complete scale for prioritized standard RI.4.7 is shown in table 2.5.

Table 2.5: Scale for RI.4.7

4.0	In addition to score 3.0 performance, the student demonstrates in-depth inferences and applications that go beyond what was taught.	
	3.5	*In addition to score 3.0 performance, partial success at score 4.0 content*
3.0	The student will interpret information presented visually, orally, or quantitatively (e.g., in charts, graphs, diagrams, time lines, animations, or interactive elements on Web pages) and explain how the information contributes to an understanding of the text in which it appears. (NGA & CCSSO, 2010a, p. 14)	
	2.5	*No major errors or omissions regarding score 2.0 content and partial success at score 3.0 content*
2.0	The student will: • Recognize and recall specific vocabulary such as *information, visual, oral, quantitative, chart, graph, time line, animation, interactive, webpage,* and *text* • Identify patterns in information presented visually, orally, or quantitatively (such as sequence, comparison, and cause and effect) • Recognize connections between figures and tables in a text and the text itself	
	1.5	*Partial success at score 2.0 content and major errors or omissions regarding score 3.0 content*
1.0	With help, partial success at score 2.0 content and score 3.0 content	
	0.5	*With help, partial success at score 2.0 content but not at score 3.0 content*
0.0	Even with help, no success	

Each scale should take about fifteen to thirty minutes to compose, depending on the amount of readiness skills needed and the complexity of the standard. In most cases, it takes a bit longer to create proficiency scales for secondary standards than for elementary standards. Teachers can divide scale-writing work among the members of their grade-level or course-specific team; this approach works especially well if proficiency scale work is done over the course of multiple meetings. Teachers can write their individual scales between meetings and spend their time together at the next meeting reviewing and revising the scales.

It is important to remember that leaders and teachers can adjust the proficiency scale format to meet their school's unique needs and situation. Sometimes schools will want the scale to be more specific at certain score levels (rather than simply using generic statements). Other schools may decide to use whole-point scores only. The following stories present examples of proficiency scales created by schools and districts in the United States.

Mike Knoebel, a physical education teacher in Douglas County School District in Colorado, worked with other physical education teachers to develop the following sixth-grade scale (table 2.6).

Table 2.6: Physical Education—Aerobic Exercise Scale

	Standard: The student is able to identify benefits and components of a healthy lifestyle.	
4.0	In addition to score 3.0 performance, the student demonstrates in-depth inferences and applications that go beyond what was taught.	
	3.5	*In addition to score 3.0 performance, partial success at score 4.0 content*
3.0	While engaged in tasks involving benefits and components of a healthy lifestyle, the student will: • Describe activities designated to improve and maintain aerobic endurance (for example, sprinting, Fitnessgram's PACER test, and activities such as tag, soccer, basketball, or geocaching that include continued or quick spurts of intense running) • Describe proper warm-up, conditioning, and cool-down techniques (for example, a short jog to warm up, stretching or anaerobic exercises for conditioning to target specific muscle groups, and walking and stretches to cool down)	
	2.5	*No major errors or omissions regarding score 2.0 content and partial success at score 3.0 content*
2.0	The student will: • Recognize or recall specific vocabulary such as *aerobic endurance, warm up, cool down,* and *conditioning* • Recognize and recall accurate statements about warm-up, conditioning, and cool-down activities • Recognize and recall accurate statements about activities that maintain aerobic endurance	
	1.5	*Partial success at score 2.0 content and major errors or omissions regarding score 3.0 content*
1.0	With help, partial success at score 2.0 content and score 3.0 content	
	0.5	*With help, partial success at score 2.0 content but not at score 3.0 content*
0.0	Even with help, no success	

Source: Knoebel, 2012.

Linda Stevens, an assessment director from Lake Washington School District in Washington State, helped teachers develop the following fifth-grade science scale (table 2.7).

Notice that teachers in this district made the score 4.0 content more specific (rather than using a generic statement), added descriptors to each score level (such as *exceeds standard*, *at standard*, and so on), and chose not to include half-point scores.

Table 2.7: Earth Science—Landforms Scale

Standard: Students explain how water shapes landforms.	
4 **Exceeds Standard**	The transfer of learning to more complex content and thinking (not new content), including deeper conceptual understanding and applications that go beyond what is explicitly taught in class The student will: • Predict how the processes of erosion and deposition can affect humans • Design a solution to a human problem related to erosion or deposition
3 **At Standard**	The standard or learning target—content, details, vocabulary, concepts, procedures, processes, and skills (simple and complex)—explicitly taught in class The student will: • Explain how water shapes landforms • Describe how a landform is created by water erosion (for example, a canyon) • Describe how a landform is created by deposition (for example, a delta)
2 **Approaching Standard**	Simpler content, details, vocabulary, procedures, processes, and skills, including foundational knowledge and concepts, explicitly taught in class The student will: • Define *erosion*, *deposition*, and *gravity* • Identify landforms created through the processes of water erosion and/or deposition • Identify the process that creates deltas (deposition) and canyons (erosion)
1 **Not At Standard**	With help, partial understanding of some of the simpler and more complex content, details, vocabulary, concepts, procedures, processes, and skills

Source: Adapted from Lake Washington School District, 2010.

Review Proficiency Scales

Once teachers have created scales for each of the prioritized standards, each team should review its entire set of scales for that grade level or course. At this point in the process, it may be useful to invite teachers not yet involved to participate in the review process. Their fresh perspective can help highlight inconsistencies or issues in the scales before they are presented to the whole school or district. Figure 2.2 presents a form that teachers can use to evaluate and comment on each scale.

Prioritized Standard: _____				
Criterion	Yes	No	Not Sure	Comments
The proficiency scale has a consistent format.				
The verbs and corresponding content represent a progression of complexity.				
The proficiency scale is doable. It has enough depth, yet not so much as to warrant an additional scale.				
The key vocabulary is highlighted for direct instruction.				
The sample activities or tasks seem appropriate and add clarity to the scale.				

Figure 2.2: Peer review criteria for proficiency scales.

It is normally most productive for teachers to complete the form in figure 2.2 for scales they did not write. Then, the teacher who wrote the scale makes revisions based on the feedback from the forms. In the following story, Lisa Bucciarelli wrote sample proficiency scales and then obtained feedback from an outside expert.

When Lisa was a high school world-language teacher in Elmhurst, Illinois, she sought feedback from her colleagues and from the American Council on the Teaching of Foreign Languages (ACTFL) about a set of proficiency scales she had written. Her colleagues indicated that she should ensure that each scale focused on a single aspect of the content, even if it meant creating more scales. Experts at the ACTFL advised her to make sure that her scales addressed the five Cs of teaching a foreign language: communication, culture, connections, comparisons, and communities. Based on this feedback, Lisa limited each scale to a single, focused area of the content and incorporated the ACTFL's suggested elements. Then she used the scales with students for a year before revisiting them with her team to revise further.

After the review and revisions are complete, teachers can begin aligning teaching materials and resources to the prioritized standards and proficiency scales and disseminating the information to all staff.

Aligning Teaching Materials

Aligning resources, assignments, and assessments to the prioritized standards and proficiency scales allows teachers to identify areas where resources may need to move from one grade level to another or where additional resources might be needed. It also helps teachers identify activities or assignments that do not relate to any of the prioritized standards.

First, teachers match existing resources to the appropriate sections of each proficiency scale. Teachers can work in teams or individually to match resources, writing the existing resource next to the appropriate section of each proficiency scale. This process should take about one to two hours.

Once existing resources have been matched, teachers can identify scale sections for which additional resources are needed. This part of the process will take about fifteen to twenty minutes per proficiency scale. Teachers should also independently double-check the resources list while using the proficiency scales with students for the first time or two, adding any additional ideas as they actually teach the content on the proficiency scale, and communicating additional needs to school leaders. School leaders should note where additional resources are needed and make plans to acquire appropriate resources for those areas. The following story details how teachers can align resources to the proficiency scales.

Michael Storrar and Rex Sickmiller, math teachers from Colorado Springs, Colorado, worked with their team to align their existing textbook chapters with specific levels of each proficiency scale. First, they denoted the chapter in their textbook that addressed the specific priority standard and proficiency scale. Then, they identified which pages in each chapter corresponded to 2.0 (simpler),

3.0 (target), and 4.0 (more complex) content on each proficiency scale. Table 2.8 shows a sample of their work.

Table 2.8: Connecting Resources to Proficiency Scales

	Scale 1: Slope, distance, and equation of line	Scale 2: Function evaluation	Scale 3: Reasonable graph or graphic representation	Scale 4: Graphing equations	Scale 5: Quadratics
Chapter	Chapter 1 (pages 38–45)	Chapter 2 (pages 46–51)	Chapter 4 (pages 63–78)	Chapter 5 (pages 82–100)	Chapter 7 (pages 147–163)
Score 4.0	pages 43–45	page 51	pages 77–78	pages 97–100	pages 161–163
Score 3.0	pages 40–42	pages 48–50	pages 65–76	pages 86–96	pages 155–160
Score 2.0	pages 38–39	pages 46–47	pages 63–64	pages 82–85	pages 147–154

The teachers also annotated other aligned resources—such as online tutorial videos, notes from class, and extra practice problems—to show which score level of which proficiency scale they corresponded to and posted the resources on the class webpage. These alignments provided more consistency among teachers who taught the same courses and helped students know where to look for help with specific score levels of specific proficiency scales.

Dissemination

Once prioritized standards have been identified and proficiency scales created, they should be shared with all teaching staff. Some leaders will elect to do this independently, and others will use a team approach. The following three steps can be used to disseminate prioritized standards and proficiency scales across a whole school or district:

1. **Share prioritized standards and proficiency scales—** Documents can be posted on a shared network or district website. It should be easy for teachers to find and access them. Consider creating a short video to accompany the scales that describes what they are, how they can be used, and other details regarding their implementation.

2. **Train teachers on the new documents**—Ask team members who identified prioritized standards and created proficiency scales to provide a series of trainings to acquaint teachers with the ideas and processes used during the work. Hearing firsthand from those involved in the process adds a human touch to the implementation process.

3. **Make yourself available for questions**—As a leader in this process, provide multiple opportunities for teachers and parents to ask questions and talk to you about the prioritized standards and proficiency scales. An FAQ document based on rotating review comments and teams' revision notes can also help address questions that arise repeatedly over time.

The most important consideration during dissemination is making sure that all staff members have access to the information they need and the opportunity to ask questions and give feedback about the work that was done.

Summary

Prioritized standards and proficiency scales are critical components of standards-based grading. A basic process can be used to help teams of teachers identify prioritized standards and create proficiency scales for each. Having common proficiency scales increases consistency from teacher to teacher and allows collaborative teams to align their available resources to specific outcomes for students. Once standards have been prioritized and proficiency scales created, teacher teams can design common assessments that measure students' achievement and progress on each standard.

Effective Assessments

Assessment can be defined as a systematic process used to make inferences about student learning (Popham, 2003; Roschewski, 2002; Stiggins, 1991, 2002; Wolf, 1993). Jay McTighe and Steven Ferrara (2000) stated that "the primary purpose of classroom assessment is to inform teaching and improve learning, not to sort and select students or to justify a grade" (p. 1). The Educational Testing Service (2003) agreed, explaining that "assessments should give all students an equal chance to show what they know and can do" (p. 7). Effective assessments allow educators to continuously and accurately monitor student achievement. Comprehensive assessment of student achievement involves multiple sources of evidence that are fair, valid, and reliable. Tammy Heflebower (2009) noted that the process of collecting, analyzing, and synthesizing information about students allows teachers to understand and describe students and their achievement more accurately. It also provides evidence that students are learning the prioritized standards. This same notion holds true for larger-scale assessments as well.

Improving student learning is an international focus. American students' scores on international assessments continue to lag behind the scores of students in many other nations in various academic areas. One of the key international assessments yielding these data is the Programme for International Student Assessment (PISA). Administered in sixty-five countries, PISA measures the ability of students to apply knowledge to real-life situations. Data from the assessment indicate that students from the United States are behind those from other countries regarding real-world application. For example, the 2009 PISA results show that U.S. students scored lower than students from twelve other countries in the area of science literacy. The same report showed that the United States scored lower than twenty-three countries in math literacy. These data signify that students need more instruction in applying their learning to relevant situations. In order to accomplish this, schools need to clearly define and raise their expectations for student performance (Darling-Hammond, 2010).

Assessment is an essential element of the learning process and is a critical component in moving a building or district toward standards-based grading and thus raising student performance. Classroom assessments must be aligned with prioritized standards and proficiency scales to ensure that they are accurately and fairly measuring the prioritized standards. This chapter addresses varying the types of assessments, designing high-quality assessments, successfully scoring assessments, and providing opportunities to redo assignments.

Varying the Types of Assessments

Linda Darling-Hammond (2010) shared interesting findings about countries like Finland and South Korea, who take the PISA. These countries have limited or eliminated their external testing systems in lieu of more ongoing performance assessments, which include problem solving, writing, projects, and papers. Students receive detailed feedback on a regular basis about their work. Interestingly, these countries are two that perform well on international exams, particularly the PISA. Finland ranked sixth in math, second in science, and third in reading and ranks in the top ten for all categories. South Korea ranked second in reading, sixth in science, and fourth in mathematics and also ranks in the top ten for all categories. These observations indicate that a variety of quality classroom assessments can be as effective as larger-scale external testing systems. In fact, international comparisons reveal that countries that balance performance assessments and regular feedback outperform other countries that rely heavily on state and national exams, such as the United States. Although one might argue that Finland and South Korea are dissimilar to the United States in many other ways, the results are informative.

In order to better understand the importance of balancing various types of assessments, it is important to clearly understand the nuances of various assessments. Three types are highlighted here: (1) obtrusive, (2) unobtrusive, and (3) student generated (Marzano, 2010). We then discuss how to approach assessing younger students.

Obtrusive Assessments

Obtrusive assessments require teachers to cease instruction in order to administer a test. These assessments are designed to be independently administered and scored and often require students to demonstrate their learning by describing through writing or speaking a particular set of knowledge and skills. Items are usually selected response (multiple choice, true/false, or matching) or constructed response (fill in the blank, short answer, or essay). Common examples of this kind of assessment include pencil-and-paper tests, quizzes, or verbal interview assessments (often used with younger students). Obtrusive assessments are common in most classrooms. Teachers and parents are usually familiar with obtrusive assessments because they experienced them when they were in school.

As an example of how a teacher creates and uses obtrusive assessment, consider a history teacher who has just taught students about components of conflict. He creates a paper-and-pencil test to assess the following prioritized standard: *Students will describe common elements of conflict that they have learned about while studying wars of the 20th century.* Using the proficiency scale for the standard, he first creates ten matching items that measure students' understanding of key vocabulary (score 2.0 content) related to conflict. Then he adds five multiple-choice items (one about score 2.0 content, three about score 3.0 content, and one about score 4.0 content). Finally, he composes three short constructed-response questions. Two are aligned to the score 3.0 content, and one addresses score 4.0 content. After students take the test, he notes each student's pattern of correct answers. Those who correctly answered all of the 2.0 items but none of the 3.0 or 4.0 items are at the 2.0 level. Those who answered all of the 2.0 and 3.0 items correctly are at the 3.0 level. Those who answered all items correctly are at the 4.0 level. If a student answered some items for a level correctly and some incorrectly (for example, all 2.0 items correct but only some 3.0 and 4.0 items correct), the teacher assigns a half-point score (such as 2.5). This lets him gauge each student's current score level.

Unobtrusive Assessments

Unobtrusive assessments usually occur without students' knowing they are being assessed. The instruction process is not interrupted. Often, these assessments occur when a teacher simply observes students performing skills or demonstrating knowledge from the proficiency scale and notes a score in her gradebook. For instance, a high school teacher might listen to a discussion between two students in her mathematics class and use a proficiency scale to rate their level of understanding. This type of assessment "can take place in any student-teacher interaction at the whole-class, small-group, or one-on-one level" (Ruiz-Primo & Furtak, 2007, p. 58). Teachers can also elicit student responses (reactions, clarifications, elaborations, or explanations) to acquire unobtrusive assessment information.

A probing discussion is a type of unobtrusive assessment that involves the teacher talking one-on-one with a student. As the student responds, the teacher uses questions based on the score levels of a proficiency scale to assess his or her level of understanding. Primary teachers use this form of assessment frequently, because young students are often emerging readers and writers and are less able to read tests and respond in a written format. According to Marzano (2010), "probing discussions are one of the most powerful forms of oral assessment" (p. 71). Another form of unobtrusive assessment is a performance assessment.

Performance assessments require students to demonstrate their knowledge and skills, often by completing a specific task. One study found that the use of performance assessments resulted in greater student achievement gains than other types of assessment (Black & Wiliam, 1998). Many 21st century skills and many of the thinking and reasoning skills from the Common Core State Standards (critical thinking, problem solving, and so on) are easier to measure using performance assessment formats. Although performance assessments can be obtrusive (if instruction stops for them to occur), they are normally unobtrusive, as the teacher observes the student completing a task and rates his or her performance using a proficiency scale. Examples of performance assessments include:

- Speaking in a foreign language
- Dribbling a basketball
- Creating a charcoal portrait
- Conducting a science experiment

Students who struggle with traditional exams may be more motivated by real-world, hands-on performance assessments. Performance assessments are particularly helpful when assessing students' performance at the 4.0 level of a proficiency scale, since that score level often involves applying knowledge in novel or real-world situations.

As an example of how a language arts teacher uses unobtrusive assessments, consider a class learning about text features. During a discussion, the teacher notes that a specific student is able to identify text features but cannot apply them to improve his understanding of text. Therefore, she gives that student a score of 2.0 for that skill. After providing additional instruction and practice for the student, the teacher uses a probing discussion to reassess his performance. The student is able to correctly answer several questions at the 3.0 level and one question at the 4.0 level. Therefore, the teacher gives the student a new score of 3.5 for that skill.

Student-Generated Assessments

Student-generated assessments directly involve the student in the assessment process; they require students to come up with ways to explain, demonstrate, and prove their learning to the teacher. In this type of assessment, the student suggests a way to demonstrate his or her proficiency on a prioritized standard. For most teachers, this is a shift from traditional assessment practices. In the beginning, teachers can guide students to use this type of assessment by providing several appropriate options and letting students choose one to demonstrate their learning. Marzano (2010) called student-generated assessments "the most powerful and underutilized type of assessment" (p. 75). Mary Jo Skillings and Robbin Ferrell (2000) offered anecdotal evidence that the use of student-generated assessments and rubrics led students to think more deeply about content, assess their own progress, and differentiate between a poor and an exemplary product. Student-generated assessments provide choice and increase student engagement in the classroom. This type of assessment can also pinpoint precisely what the student can and cannot do, leading to even better instructional decisions by the teacher.

Jay McTighe and Ken O'Connor (2005) offered advice about implementing student-generated assessments:

> First, teachers need to collect appropriate evidence of learning on the basis of goals rather than simply offer a "cool" menu of assessment choices. If a content standard calls for proficiency in written or oral presentations, it would be inappropriate to provide performance options other than those involving writing or speaking, except in the case of students for whom such goals are clearly inappropriate (a newly arrived English language learner, for example). Second, the options must be worth the time and energy required. It would be inefficient to have students develop an elaborate three-dimensional display or an animated PowerPoint presentation for content that a multiple-choice quiz could easily assess. . . . Third, teachers have only so much time and energy, so they must be judicious in determining when it is important to offer product and performance options. They need to strike a healthy balance between a single assessment path and a plethora of choices. (p. 15)

Student-generated assessments provide many options for students. For example, a student who scored 2.5 on a traditional test involving causes of the Civil War might ask the teacher if she could produce a short video clip to show understanding at the 3.0 level after doing additional reading. A math student who made several errors on a test involving quadratic equations could practice the concept and have a probing discussion with the teacher that showed his mastery of the process. In both situations, proficiency scales guide the teacher to determine the student's competence with newly acquired knowledge and skills.

Performance assessments or probing discussions with the teacher can be used as student-generated assessments as long as the student chooses that type of assessment to display his or her knowledge and skills. Options that are less formal and structured can include student-generated questions, student-created checklists, or choice boards. Student-generated questions involve students creating comprehensive questions and responses that capture the key concepts learned. A student-created checklist involves students creating a list of key components that must be demonstrated in a written piece or shared verbally with the teacher. Choice boards look like a matrix with options that the teacher (or student) created for a specific prioritized standard. Figure 3.1 (page 42) shows one example of a choice board (designed to assess students' skill with identifying story elements), where students choose three options to form a Tic-Tac-Toe line. Each row of the Tic-Tac-Toe grid corresponds to a different cognitive level (2.0, 3.0, or 4.0). For example, the top row asks students to describe characters, the middle row addresses students' understanding of setting and plot, and the bottom row prompts students to relate the elements of one story to those of a different story. A teacher could require students to select one box from each row or, to assess a particular level of thinking, multiple boxes from the same row.

Create finger puppets with the features of the story's characters.	Draw a picture that shows what each character in the story looks like.	Use an audio app (like Jing) to verbally describe the characters.
Use a social learning platform (like Edmodo) to respond to teacher prompts and participate in student discussions about the story's setting and plot.	Keep a scrapbook to show the characters, setting, and plot of the story.	Write a descriptive paragraph about the characters, setting, and plot of the story.
Make a collage or storyboard depicting the story's characters, setting, and plot and connect each element to another story with a similar plot.	Sing a song or create a rap about the key elements of the story and how it relates to another story with similar elements.	Design a board game that highlights the characters, setting, and plot of this story and another story with similar story elements.

Figure 3.1: Tic-Tac-Toe choice board.

As an example of how a teacher could use student-generated assessments, consider a physical education teacher at a middle school. If a student scored lower than he wanted to on an endurance test that involved running a certain number of laps in a set amount of time, he would improve his endurance and then ask to run the laps again to demonstrate his increased level of fitness.

Assessments for Young Students

The key to assessing young students is understanding how to effectively use various types of assessments (obtrusive, unobtrusive, and student generated). When assessing young students, it is important to have valid and reliable assessments, but some assessments are difficult for young students because they are just learning how to read and write. It would be incorrect to assume that a first grader does not understand a concept simply because he or she cannot write a descriptive paragraph about it. Asking younger students to talk about their knowledge and skills is often more accurate and separates their ability to write from their understanding of knowledge or skills. Similarly, if a student scores poorly on an assessment because he or she couldn't read the directions, the teacher will not obtain an accurate representation of that student's knowledge and skill with the prioritized standard.

Designing High-Quality Assessments

Effective assessment development is important regardless of the type of assessment being used. In the same way that teachers need to understand the criteria for prioritizing standards and the format of a generic proficiency scale before completing the work described in chapter 2, they need to understand *levels of thinking* before they can create quality classroom assessments.

Levels of thinking describe the degrees of cognition required for an assessment. For example, is the student being asked to list three causes of the Civil War, or is he being asked to describe each cause in detail? The former requires a student to simply know three causes of the Civil War and list them. The latter requires the student to know three causes of the Civil War and also provide a detailed description of each, making it a more difficult task. Identifying the level of thinking for each item on an assessment allows teachers to more accurately assess students' current knowledge or skill for a prioritized standard.

Creating items at different levels of thinking is relatively easy when using a proficiency scale, because proficiency scales detail differences between simpler and target content and skills. It is important to ensure that items at various levels of thinking are included on each assessment. Score 2.0 assessment items should require less complex thinking from a student than score 3.0 items. A student who can describe an isosceles triangle or select it from a vocabulary list (score 2.0) might not be able to compare and contrast an isosceles triangle to a scalene or equilateral triangle (score 3.0). If a teacher only puts items on an exam that assess score 3.0 performance, then he or she will only know whether or not a student has obtained mastery of score 3.0 knowledge and skills. The teacher does not know if the student knows any of the score 2.0 simpler content because no items on the exam measured that content. Conversely, if an advanced student took the same exam and there were no score 4.0 items, the teacher would have no way of knowing that the advanced student had deeper understanding than the score 3.0 items required. In short, including items at various levels of thinking allows a teacher to measure students' performance in greater detail. Even primary teachers should align interview or demonstration questions asked of young students with the proficiency scales.

A common misconception about levels of thinking is that a specific level of thinking can be denoted by specific verbs. For example, the verbs *explain* and *analyze* are often considered higher-level verbs. However, this does not hold true in an assessment item like "*Explain* to me where you live," which requires a simple rote response. Similarly, "*Analyze* this sentence to decide if the commas have been used correctly" does not require higher-level cognitive processing. If a student has learned the rules for using commas, he or she is merely recalling and applying the rule. Neither example requires interaction with the content on a deeper level. To further illustrate the unreliability of verbs when considering levels of thinking, consider table 3.1 (page 44).

In table 3.1, the same verb, *describe*, is used in all three examples, but each use requires different levels of thinking for student success. It is the pairing of the verb with content that increases the thinking complexity. Thus, it is important for teachers to get peer feedback about their initial alignment and make adjustments based on comments and questions from other teachers.

Table 3.1: Increasing Levels of Thinking Using a Single Verb

	Simple Cognitive Demand	**Complex Cognitive Demand**	**More Complex Cognitive Demand**
Describe	Describe three characteristics of metamorphic rocks.	Describe the difference between metamorphic and igneous rocks.	Describe a model that represents the relationships that exist within the rock cycle.
Level of thinking	Requires simple recall.	Requires cognitive processing to determine the differences in the two rock types.	Requires deep understanding of the rock cycle and a determination of how best to represent it.

There are several ways teachers can use their understanding of levels of thinking to design high-quality assessments: they can create new assessments that directly align to the levels denoted on the proficiency scales, modify existing assessments to validate previous work and possibly lessen the load of assessment-item writing, or use common assessments.

New Assessments

Like identifying prioritized standards and creating proficiency scales, it is crucial that *teachers* do the work of creating new assessments because it is important that they understand the underlying concepts and processes involved in creating quality assessments. James McMillan, Steve Myran, and Daryl Workman (2002) explained,

> The existing literature on elementary classroom assessment practices indicates that teachers probably need further training to improve the quality of the assessments that are used. Whatever the type of question used on assessments, few are written to tap students' higher level thinking skills. (p. 204)

Anne Lewis (1996) suggested that teachers be the center of assessment activities—embedding assessments in their instruction, scoring the assessments, and discussing standards for good student work with colleagues, parents, and students. Otherwise, poorly developed assessments are likely to become a distraction and source of frustration (Gandal & Vranek, 2001).

As explained in the discussion of levels of thinking, assessment items must align with the proficiency scales. This ensures that the items on the exam actually measure the expected content and process knowledge. Sometimes, teachers grade students using activities or assessment items that have nothing to do with the actual content or process information on the proficiency scale. For example, if a language arts teacher assessing students' ability to compare and contrast different types of nonfiction asks students to create a costume for one of the characters in a nonfiction text and present the costume to the class, there is a mismatch between the assessment and the proficiency scale. Instead, teachers should use their proficiency scales to create the assessment items for each score level. Consider a seventh-grade math teacher who uses a proficiency scale to determine what knowledge and skills his students should master during a particular unit. The 2.0, 3.0, and 4.0 levels of such a scale are shown in table 3.2.

Table 3.2: Seventh-Grade Proficiency Scale for Ratios and Unit Rates

4.0	In addition to score 3.0 performance, the student demonstrates in-depth inferences and applications that go beyond what was taught.
3.0	The student will "compute unit rates associated with ratios of fractions . . . measured in like or different units" (7.RP.1; NGA & CCSSO, 2010b, p. 48).
2.0	The student will recognize or recall specific vocabulary, such as: • *Compute, fraction, like, ratio, unit, unit rate, unlike* The student will perform basic processes, such as: • Decide whether two quantities are in a proportional relationship (7.RP.2a; NGA & CCSSO, 2010b, p. 48)

First, he plans how many items he will need for each level of the scale and decides on seven 2.0 vocabulary matching items, one 2.0 item for deciding whether two quantities are in a proportional relationship, three 3.0 items that ask students to compute unit rates, and one 4.0 item that uses the 3.0 concepts in a real-world situation. The assessment blueprint in table 3.3 illustrates this plan.

Table 3.3: Assessment Blueprint

Scale Descriptor	**2.0**	**3.0**	**4.0**
The student will recognize or recall specific vocabulary, such as: • *Compute, fraction, like, ratio, unit, unit rate, unlike*	7 matching items		
The student will perform basic processes, such as: • Decide whether two quantities are in a proportional relationship	1 short-answer item		
The student will compute unit rates associated with ratios of fractions measured in like or unlike units		3 short-answer items	
In addition to score 3.0 performance, the student demonstrates in-depth inferences and applications that go beyond what was taught. For example, the student will find the best deal on soda sold at the local market by comparing various unit rates and figuring various taxes when purchasing the soda in various counties and states.			1 extended-response item

As he scores his students' exams, the teacher examines which assessment items each of his students completed correctly or incorrectly. This detailed assessment information helps him plan instruction, remediation, and extensions for each student.

Once teachers have created assessment items representing various levels of thinking, they must make sure the assessment is free of bias. This check requires teachers to understand what biased items look like and the reasons that items may be perceived as biased for some subgroups of students. There are several types of biased assessment components: controversial content, poor directions, items that rely on student experiences outside of school, unfair representation of certain subgroups, and poor formatting. Controversial content might be an issue if a teacher uses a word problem that involves gambling with dice on a ratios assessment when some students or their parents object to the use of dice or gambling references. Directions that use unfamiliar terms (such as *formulate* or *analyze*) not used regularly in class can also create bias. If the directions for an assessment are not clear or use unfamiliar words, students may have to guess about what they are being asked to do rather than clearly understand how to approach an assessment item. One of the most common forms of assessment bias involves items that rely on students' experiences outside of school for success. For example, a descriptive writing prompt that asks students to write about the state they live in may be especially difficult for students who just moved to that state, simply because of their limited experiences, even if they have a firm grasp of the components of descriptive writing. Unfair representation of certain subgroups refers to test items that either favor or eliminate certain ethnic names or examples. For example, if a student is of Hispanic descent, yet only sees Anglo-American–derived names on an exam, he or she may underperform due to the lack of representation. Finally, poor formatting can also cause students to underperform. If there is only a small amount of white space under a question, students may limit their responses to fit only within that space, even if it means not sharing the full extent of their knowledge and skills. By having other teachers review assessments, by requesting and reviewing feedback from students, and by paying close attention to discrepancies between students' expected and actual performance on an assessment, teachers can avoid these potential sources of bias.

Teachers should also evaluate an assessment after giving it for the first time, reflecting on how students performed on each item and revising as necessary. One way to do this is to ask students to write anything that was particularly confusing or frustrating about the format on the back of the exam. Another way is for the teacher to actually take the assessment to identify resources that students will need or awkwardly worded questions. Alternatively, teachers can make predictions (based on other assessment data) about how specific students will score on the assessment and see if those predictions come true. For example, if a teacher expects a student to get level 3.0 items correct (based on his performance in class discussions and feedback from homework) and the student gets all the level 3.0 items correct, it is a good indicator that the assessment is accurately measuring students' performance.

In addition to eliminating bias in assessment items, teachers need to be sure that assessment items and corresponding directions are written at an appropriate readability level for students. For example, an eighth-grade assessment should have items written at an eighth-grade readability level. There are several ways to determine the readability level of an assessment item. If an assessment item was created by a textbook or assessment publisher or assessment company, there may be documents available on the company's website reporting the readability level of the item. If not, use the Flesch-Kincaid Readability Analysis found in Microsoft Office's Word software (versions 2007, 2010; Mac versions 2008, 2011). When checking spelling and grammar, click on the Options button in the Spelling and Grammar dialog box and check the box next to "Show readability statistics" in the window that opens. When Word finishes checking the spelling and grammar of the document, it will display statistics about the grade level and readability of the document. It is also helpful to have teachers who teach the same grade level review items' readability to discern their appropriateness.

Existing Assessments

Effective assessment items can also be developed by drawing on existing assessments. The backmapping process involves reviewing an existing assessment and the corresponding proficiency scale to determine if the items on the assessment match the levels of performance defined by the proficiency scale. If a school or district already has common assessments, backmapping is a good alternative to creating new assessments. Additionally, using existing assessments validates previous work and affirms to those involved in the earlier assessment development processes that components are worth saving.

When backmapping existing assessments to new proficiency scales, teachers may discover that the existing items do not exactly match the content in the proficiency scale or that all the items apply to only a single level of the proficiency scale. If all of the items on an existing assessment pertain to the score 2.0 level of the proficiency scale, the assessment is probably too easy. If all the items pertain to the 4.0 level, the assessment is probably too difficult. If all the items pertain to the 3.0 level, teachers will not be able to collect meaningful data about students who may be at the 2.0 or 4.0 levels of the scale. Backmapping assessments often involves adding more of a specific level of item to the assessment or discarding some of the existing assessment items.

The process of backmapping an existing assessment has four steps:

1. Teachers identify the proficiency scale or scales that need to be measured by the existing assessment.

2. Teachers examine each assessment item to determine the level of the proficiency scale that it corresponds with and label it appropriately.

3. Teachers identify assessment items that do not correspond to any levels of the proficiency scale and remove them.

4. Teachers add items for levels of the proficiency scale not represented by items already on the assessment.

Backmapping is extremely important if teachers use item banks (either free or those that accompany curriculum materials) to obtain items for assessments. Each item taken from an item bank should be reviewed to determine its corresponding level on the proficiency scale. Teachers should use caution with items that come with predetermined designations about their levels. These items should always be evaluated against the specific proficiency scale for the assessment being created.

Sometimes items on a single assessment will correspond to multiple proficiency scales (and therefore to multiple prioritized standards). Table 3.4 shows an example of how items on an existing mathematics assessment could be classified by their score level and related prioritized standard and proficiency scale.

Table 3.4: Assessment Classification of Items

Prioritized Standard/ Proficiency Scale	Proficiency Scale Level	Existing Item Number(s)
Students divide multidigit numbers efficiently and effectively.	2.0	1, 2
	3.0	3, 4, 5
	4.0	6
Students solve single- and multistep word problems involving multidigit division and verify solutions.	2.0	7, 8
	3.0	9, 10, 11
	4.0	12, 13

To address multiple proficiency scales on a single assessment, teachers can break the assessment into sections that reference different prioritized standards or break the assessment into two separate assessments. The following story explains one district's experience backmapping assessments.

> Linda Stevens found that when teachers learned how to backmap assessments, they were surprised to find that the assessments that often came with the curriculum were not already leveled. Now, when new materials are purchased, Linda and other district leaders bring small groups of teachers together to level items with the district's proficiency scales. In some cases, Linda and her team develop alignment guides for purchased materials and provide them to teachers.

Common Assessments

While teachers can write or backmap assessments individually, sharing the work is more efficient and creates consistency from teacher to teacher and course to course. Assessments created and used by a grade-level or content-area team are often referred to as *common assessments*. Common assessments are defined as assessments that are administered routinely by a group of teachers to measure student academic achievement, including statewide assessments, end-of-course tests, and interim tests (Hamilton et al., 2009). There are several potential benefits of common assessments, including clarification of learning targets and performance standards, collaborative contributions to interpret results, and sharing of ideas about instructional modifications to improve learning (Fisher & Kopenski, 2008; Kanold & Ebert, 2010; Supovitz & Christman, 2003).

Common assessments are typically obtrusive because the conditions for the assessment (amount of time, directions, number and type of examples) need to be the same from one teacher to another. To create common assessments, teacher teams must plan how many items will be included for each score level. Then, each teacher on the team creates items to contribute to the common assessment. Some teams divide the work by having certain teammates write score 2.0 items, others write score 3.0 items, and still others write score 4.0 items. Other teams assign a range of items to each teammate. After items are created, the team reviews them for appropriate levels of thinking, absence of bias, and readability. The team then compiles the items into an assessment and administers it to students. After administering the assessment, the teachers regroup to discuss instructional next steps. Richard DuFour and Robert Marzano (2011) explained,

> Immediately after the assessment is administered, members of the team analyze the results to determine appropriate actions they can take in class and to identify students who require additional support through the school's system of intervention. Thus, the common assessment provides focused data used by team members to optimize their instructional effectiveness. (p. 133)

The following story describes how a world-language team collaborated to create common assessments.

> Lisa Bucciarelli created common assessments with her teammates. Assessments used before the creation of prioritized standards and proficiency scales were revisited and backmapped for reliability and validity. She said, "We reviewed each common assessment to ensure each test item measured what we intended it to measure. . . . We did so by looking at each item, denoting which level of proficiency it aligned to and if there were any concerns with how the item was written." During these reviews, the team created an assessment blueprint that denoted how many questions were related to each level of each proficiency scale.

Successfully Scoring Assessments

Scoring guides should be created after assessments are created and should include the title of the assessment, directions for the assessment, guidance to teachers about examples to use with the class prior to the assessment, and guidance about what constitutes a correct or incorrect response for each item (that is, an answer key).

Scoring guides are an important component of high-quality assessments, especially good common assessments, since they ensure fairness in assessment practices, provide more reliable interpretations of assessment information, and allow for more consistency in administration and scoring. These guides also help each teacher understand which items assess which proficiency level and how to identify correct, partially correct, and incorrect responses.

DuFour and Marzano (2011) explained a coding system that teachers can use in conjunction with a scoring guide to code student responses on assessments as correct, incorrect, or partially correct:

- C = completely correct (all elements of the item are correct)
- NC = completely incorrect (no elements of the item are correct)
- LP = low partial (some, but not the majority, of the item's elements are correct)
- HP = high partial (most, but not all, of the item's elements are correct)

Scoring items in this manner allows a teacher to see a pattern of student responses and corresponding areas of strength and weakness. Consider a teacher who has just administered an assessment with twelve items. Each item corresponds to a specific score level on the proficiency scale. The teacher codes each item as correct (C), not correct (NC), or partial credit (LP or HP). Table 3.5 shows how a teacher might do this. After coding each item on the assessment, the teacher examines the pattern of responses to determine the student's current status. Based on the student's responses in table 3.5, the teacher infers that the student is at the 2.5 level (all 2.0 items correct but only partial credit for 3.0 items).

Table 3.5: Scoring Guide

Item	Proficiency Scale Level	Correct?
1	2.0	C
2	2.0	C
3	2.0	C
4	2.0	C
5	3.0	LP
6	3.0	HP
7	3.0	HP
8	3.0	NC
9	3.0	LP
10	3.0	LP
11	4.0	NC
12	4.0	NC

The following stories explain two districts' experiences with scoring guides as a way to ensure consistency in how directions are shared, the number and types of examples used, and other factors that contribute to reliable assessment administration.

> Jennifer Murdock, a first-grade teacher in Castle Rock, Colorado, and her team decided to use a scoring guide during their reading assessment. The teachers on her team agreed to look at each question they would pose to students after the reading to ensure they were asking the same questions. They also agreed on one prompt they would each use if a student seemed confused by the initial question. Finally, they agreed on the amount of time they would allow for each question and student response. Because Jennifer and her team used very specific guidelines when administering their common assessment, they found that they got more reliable data from the assessment. Also, they spent less time discussing differences in how they administered the test and more time focusing on remediation and extension strategies for their low-scoring students.
>
> Linda Stevens said that scoring guides had changed her teachers' expectations: "An interesting phenomenon happens when districts provide scoring guides for assessments—teachers love them and come to expect them everywhere. If proficiency scales and leveled assessments are the 'bread and butter' of a good system of proficiency, then scoring guides are the jam—the part teachers love the best!" For Linda's district, scoring guides provided clarity about each test question on the test by delineating the level of rigor of each question, the correct answer, and all of the possible things to look for on the constructed-response questions. She said, "Scoring guides took the mystery out of scoring and created consistency."

Providing Opportunities to Redo Assignments

Reassessment means providing students with multiple opportunities to demonstrate understanding of a prioritized standard. Obtrusive, unobtrusive, or student-generated assessments can all be used as reassessments. The goal of quality assessment is to obtain information from a student about his or her journey toward mastery of prioritized standards. Reassessments allow students to continue that journey if they fail to attain mastery on an initial assessment. While some might argue that the real world does not give second chances, this is not actually the case. Many very important tests can be taken repeatedly. Lawyers retake the bar exam, high school students regularly take the SAT or ACT more than once, and drivers can retake the driving test until they pass. Reassessment helps students understand that learning, rather than a grade, is most important.

Mastery may take longer for some students, and other students may simply need multiple opportunities to demonstrate their knowledge and skills. Many students who have given up on themselves and their schools reengage in learning when teachers use reassessment. Robert Marzano, Debra Pickering, and Jane Pollock (2001) found that when students were reassessed until they demonstrated proficiency, it resulted in an effect size of 0.53, which translates to a 20 percentile point gain. Reassessment is an important part of an environment where standards can and must be met and where students are not permitted to submit substandard work without being asked to revise.

Many teachers object to reassessment because they feel that if students know they can retake an assignment or test, they won't take it seriously the first time. Indeed, it would be poor practice to allow students to simply hand in an assignment a second time or take the test at a later date without making an attempt to learn more. McTighe and O'Connor (2005) explained how teachers can address these concerns:

> Students may not take the first attempt seriously once they realize they'll have a second chance. In addition, teachers often become overwhelmed by the logistical challenges of providing multiple opportunities. To make this approach effective, teachers need to require their students to provide some evidence of the corrective action they will take—such as engaging in peer coaching, revising their report, or practicing the needed skill in a given way—before embarking on their "second chance." (p. 17)

A student should demonstrate evidence of new knowledge or skills learned before having another opportunity to show mastery. Some teachers require students to take part in specific study sessions or minilessons prior to retaking a test. Others ask students to complete additional problems to describe their new learning or have students reflect on why they did poorly the first time, either in writing or in a conversation with the teacher. Without such expectations, students may not give their best effort on the initial assessment or assignment.

As with initial assessments, proficiency scales should guide reassessment. It is also sound practice to use a different form (obtrusive, unobtrusive, or student generated) of the test for the retest whenever possible. For example, if a teacher observes a primary student who previously scored low on an obtrusive assessment correctly using verb tenses in a discussion, he might denote a new score for that student using the appropriate proficiency scale (unobtrusive assessment). Some districts have created their own item banks of various leveled assessment items (for scores 2.0, 3.0, and 4.0), which allow teachers to create multiple versions of an exam.

Regardless of the type of assessment used, students should track their own progress on each prioritized standard over time. This can be as simple as having the student create a bar or line graph of the scores he achieved on all of the activities, assignments, and assessments related to one learning goal. If a student redoes an assignment or retakes a test, she graphs the retest score in addition to previous scores. As scores improve (as should be the case with extra work, tutoring sessions, and other interventions), students can see how their additional effort has resulted in improved achievement. Figure 3.2 shows how one student tracked her progress. In this case, the student completed three assignments for one learning goal and then took a test, scoring a 2.5. After a study session and an additional assignment, the student retook the test (using an alternate form) and was able to score at the 3.0 level.

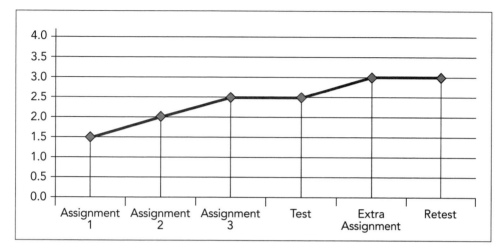

Figure 3.2: Student progress over time.

Seeing the relationship graphically helps students understand how effort and achievement are related. Marzano and Pickering (2011) pointed out that an important part of engagement involves a student believing that he or she can do what is expected. When students receive feedback about their academic performance that is connected graphically with their effort and participation, they see a stronger connection between what they do and how they perform.

The following stories describe how three teachers gave students opportunities for reassessment.

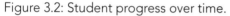

Kristin Poage, a middle school language arts teacher in Blooming-ton, Indiana, described a colleague's approach to reassessment. The teacher gave students a problem to complete on individual dry-erase boards. As she walked around the room and observed, the teacher noticed that one of her students was struggling in the area of long division. The teacher pulled the student aside for a short minilesson and asked him to complete two assessment items from the district's item bank. After his additional learning, he was successful with both.

Michael Storrar required students to prove that their learning had increased before giving them an opportunity for reassessment. Some students participated in additional learning sessions, either online or in person, before being reassessed. Others completed additional assignments or reading before reassessment. The data generated as a result of reassessments and the number of times students needed reassessment opportunities were used to make informed decisions about pacing, where additional learning units were needed, and which teachers would create online supplements. Discussions during PLC team meetings were centered on specific skills and skill gaps and how to address any deficiencies that were highlighted.

Peter Richey, a middle school mathematics teacher in Elmhurst, Illinois, had a student he thought could perform better academically. To help, he asked the student to track not only his academic progress, but also the amount of time he put into studying concepts from class each day and how much time he put into reviewing skills during the week. After one week, the student showed the teacher the results. He had spent no time that week studying outside of class and consequently failed that week's quiz. The teacher asked the student to try something different. He asked him to try studying each afternoon for fifteen minutes—simply reviewing notes and reworking problems from class. After the week's quiz, Mr. Richey and the student reviewed the graph of the student's scores and effort. The student immediately saw the correlation between increased effort and increased scores. Adding a small amount of effort into his daily routine led to significant improvement in his weekly quiz grade.

Summary

Ensuring the use of quality classroom assessments is an important component of standards-based grading. Teachers should understand and use all types of assessments (obtrusive, unobtrusive, and student generated) when determining what students know and are able to do. It is also important to ensure that the assessments are valid, reflect appropriate levels of thinking, are free from bias, and are written at the appropriate reading level. Teachers can either create new assessment items, create common assessments, or backmap existing assessments to the proficiency scales. Redoing assignments and retaking tests are instrumental in providing students with multiple opportunities for success, and when coupled with tracking progress, student achievement increases. By employing these elements, educators can be more confident about each student's level of performance on the prioritized standards. In chapter 4, we explore how teachers can use proficiency scales and assessments to assign meaningful grades.

Meaningful Grades

Using proficiency scales and a variety of assessments based on prioritized standards, teachers can assign grades that are valid and consistent. In many existing grading systems, teachers assign grades using personal philosophies and individually created rubrics. This lack of consistency can frustrate students, parents, and teachers. Using proficiency scales means that it does not matter which teacher a student has for algebra; because all algebra teachers use the same assessments and proficiency scales, they all have the same expectations for competence. When every teacher uses the same criteria to assign grades, students receive a consistent message about what is expected of them. To reap these benefits, schools should use common proficiency scales and common assessments to assign grades.

As a school implements standards-based grading, it is important for students and their parents to understand the changes and the new system, such as how grades are determined and what actions students can take to improve their grades. Parents are often concerned about changes to a grading system because grades play such an important role in class ranks, grade point averages, scholarship awards, and other important factors that contribute to students' success in college and careers. In this chapter, we review the nuts and bolts of determining students' grades in a standards-based system.

The technique of averaging students' scores for a unit, semester, quarter, or other period of time to obtain a single score is one traditional way to determine a student's overall or final grade. Other methods for determining grades include using the median score (sequentially ordering scores and using the middle one) or the mode score (the most frequently occurring score in a set of scores). Another practice is to use a trend score (which estimates the difference between a student's actual score and expected score). We assert that there are more accurate ways to arrive at grades that clearly communicate students' learning and current status on prioritized standards.

Students should know what they need to do to be successful and what actions they can take to improve their grades. Basing students' grades on proficiency scales works well because it allows students to see the connection between what they are to learn (prioritized standards), how they are learning it (classroom activities and assignments), and how they are being assessed (proficiency scales). The first step is for teachers to clearly delineate the proficiency score that each instructional activity or assignment and each assessment task correspond to. An alignment chart, as seen in table 4.1, can be used for this purpose.

Table 4.1: Alignment Chart

Score	Goal Statement	Instructional Activities and Assignments	Assessment Tasks
4.0	In addition to score 3.0 performance, the student demonstrates in-depth inferences and applications that go beyond what was taught.	The student reads real-life examples of using rounding of whole numbers in real-world context. With teacher-directed discussion, explicit connections are taught and noted.	The student explains how rounding whole numbers to the nearest 10 and 100 help in figuring a family's grocery bill. The student cites other real-life examples, including explanations of how rounding whole numbers saves time and provides information.
3.0	The student will "use place value understanding to round whole numbers to the nearest 10 or 100" (3.NBT.1; NGA & CCSSO, 2010b, p. 24).	The student will draw three cards from a deck of cards in which the non-number cards have been removed. The student will write down those numbers on a piece of paper to form a three-digit number. He or she will round that three-digit number to the nearest 10 and 100.	The student will solve three-digit place value problems on a pencil-and-paper test. Sample questions include: 900 + 50 + _____ = 955 3 + _____ + 300 = 393 The student will solve rounding problems on a pencil-and-paper test. Sample questions include: Round 421 to the nearest hundred. Round 956 to the nearest thousand. Please add the rounded numbers from the two previous problems together. The total is _____.
2.0	The student will recognize or recall specific vocabulary, such as *nearest*, *place value*, *round*, and *whole number*. The student will use place value understanding to round whole numbers below 1,000 to the nearest 10 and 100 with visual support.	The student will complete a mix-and-match vocabulary game to review key terms. The student will use visual supports such as pictures to round three-digit numbers to the nearest 10 and 100.	The student will match vocabulary terms to their correct descriptions. The student will match a three-digit number to pictures representing the number rounded to the nearest 10 and 100.

As students accumulate scores, it is important for teachers to give them feedback about their progress. In chapter 3, we discussed how students can create line graphs of their scores. Alternatively, a teacher could ask students to use highlighters to denote their progress and current status on a copy of the current unit's proficiency scale. For example, a fifth-grade student highlights where he is on the proficiency scale for the mathematics prioritized standard currently being taught and takes that copy of the proficiency scale home to share with his parents. Additionally, a teacher can use a proficiency scale when conducting student-led or parent-teacher conferences to clearly describe how a student's grade was derived and what the grade communicates about the student's learning in the classroom. The following stories illustrate how two educators helped their students understand how grades were determined.

Jeff Flygare made grades more meaningful for his students by helping them understand how their grades were computed. Using a proficiency scale, he communicated exactly what was expected of students on each assignment or assessment. He also explained how students' scores during a unit were used to assign their summative grades at the end of a unit. When students understood more clearly what was expected on each assignment and how their grades were computed, they felt more ownership for both their learning and their grades. In his AP English Literature and Composition class, Jeff sorted all of the instructional activities and assessments he used in the course according to which prioritized standard and proficiency scale they related to. He found that some of the activities and assignments he had used for years didn't align with any of the standards or scale levels, so he focused his time in class on only those activities and assessments that aligned with the scales.

Kristin Poage found that clear and honest feedback was crucial to making students' grades more meaningful. On each assignment, Kristin explicitly stated the prioritized standard in terms her students could understand. She fully explained each prioritized standard to students. "After all," she said, "how can we expect students to know what to do if we don't explain it clearly to them?" Kristin's colleague, Mrs. Kent, started giving directions on her assignments that explicitly stated what students needed to know or be able to do to receive a 3.0 score. Instead of "On your paper, write a paragraph about what goals you have for seventh grade. Include as many details as possible," Mrs. Kent wrote the following:

Prioritized Standard: 7.4.2 Paragraph Organization

On your paper, please do the following to receive a 3.0 score:

- Write fifty to seventy-five words about a goal you have for your seventh-grade year of school.

- Write a topic sentence clearly stating your goal.
- Give three specific details about how you will accomplish this goal.

The clearly stated goals let students know exactly what was required of them and gave Mrs. Kent a clear set of grading guidelines to follow.

Determining Grades

Once activities, assignments, and assessments have been aligned to proficiency scales, teachers assign scores to students based on how closely their performance matches the levels and descriptors on the proficiency scales. When it is time to report a student's overall grade for a unit of study or period of time, we recommend that teachers use the following guidelines rather than simply computing an average score.

1. Examine the student's performance on assignments and assessments.

2. Give more weight to recent information (that is, information from later in the unit).

3. If necessary, discuss the content with the student to shed light on his or her learning progress.

4. Limit the use of zero.

These four guidelines can help teachers assign grades to students accurately and fairly.

Examine Performance on Assignments and Assessments

A student's scores across the activities, assignments, and assessments used during a unit constitute the main body of information a teacher should consider when determining the student's final grade. These data might include scores from unobtrusive assessments (such as informal conversations held between the teacher and the student) or student-generated assessments. Because any single measure of learning can be unreliable, we recommend using several indicators to determine students' grades.

Marzano (2010) stated, "The average of the formative scores should not be used as the summative score, nor should the final score in the set of scores be automatically assigned as the summative score" (p. 81). Rather, teachers should consider a body of evidence. A simple average may adversely penalize a student for scoring low early in the unit before he or she had learned the content. Conversely, one bad test at the end should not completely derail an otherwise proficient pattern of evidence.

There is one instance in which averaging is appropriate. After summative scores for individual prioritized standards have been determined, it is appropriate to average those summative scores to obtain an overall grade for a subject area. For example, if summative scores were assigned for three prioritized ELA standards during a quarter, a teacher could average those three summative scores to express the student's overall achievement for ELA. So, if a student scored 3.0 on prioritized standard 1 in ELA, 2.5 on prioritized standard 2 in ELA, and 2.5 on prioritized standard 3 in ELA, then averaging those scores to obtain 2.67 would provide a legitimate measure of his or her overall performance in ELA.

Weight Recent Information

Guskey (2002) recommended that teachers seek out the information that gives the most accurate picture of a student's current status for a prioritized standard. Often, this information is the most recent information from that student. For example, if a student started with a 1.5, then scored a 2.5, then a 3.0 on the same prioritized standard, the most recent score of 3.0 is likely to be the most accurate indicator of the student's status for that prioritized standard.

Discuss Content Further With Students

Although unlikely, there may be instances in which a student's scores dip downward at the end of a unit, resulting in higher scores at the beginning of a unit and lower scores at the end. When these abnormal patterns occur, it is important to seek additional information from students before determining their final grade at the end of a unit. Ideally, the teacher will be able to determine the reason for the decline and address it. Often, a declining pattern of scores may indicate misunderstanding of a key concept or an emotional-behavioral issue that needs to be addressed in order for the student to reengage in learning. A good method for collecting this additional information is unobtrusive or student-generated assessments. These assessments give students another opportunity to demonstrate their proficiency on a prioritized standard. For instance, a student may demonstrate proficiency on a class assignment but not perform well on a quiz a few days later. When the teacher checks in with the student, she realizes that the wording used on the quiz was confusing for the student, causing a decrease in his performance. Other causes for unexpected declines in student performance include lack of practice for more difficult skills or poor study habits and organizational skills.

Limit the Use of Zero

The traditional grading practice of using a zero to indicate incomplete work is antithetical to standards-based grading. Heflebower (2009) instructed schools and districts to

> examine the unfairness and poor practice of giving zeros—of assuming that students know nothing because their assignments are overdue or missing. This is not to say that such lack of student

responsibility should be encouraged; it certainly should not be. However, we must separate student work habits from their academic achievement. (p. 127)

If a teacher wants to be truly focused on student learning, giving zeros for incomplete assignments is in direct contrast to this fundamental purpose. Some teachers defend the practice of assigning zeros by arguing that they cannot give students credit for work that is incomplete or not turned in, and that is certainly an issue. Yet, as Guskey (2002) explained, "there are far better ways to motivate and encourage students to complete assignments than by assigning them zeroes" (p. 779).

In a standards-based classroom, students should receive a *no mark* (NM) or *incomplete* (INC) in the gradebook for a missing assignment. This sends the message that students must complete the assigned work; they cannot skip assignments and "take a zero" for them. A systematic process should be set up in the classroom for students who struggle or need extra accountability for their work. School leaders could create a workshop time when students who have not turned work in, or who have struggled, can receive intervention directly with their teacher. As a reward, students who have turned all of their work in and are on target to meet their goals can participate in an enrichment activity. On a teacher team, one teacher could work with students who need intervention while the others lead enrichment time. In this situation, each team member would have an intervention period alternating with one or more enrichment periods. Table 4.2 presents an example of how this might work.

Table 4.2: Sample Schedule for Workshop Time for a Three-Person Teacher Team

Week 1	Week 2	Week 3
Teacher A = Intervention	Teacher A = Enrichment	Teacher A = Enrichment
Teacher B = Enrichment	Teacher B = Intervention	Teacher B = Enrichment
Teacher C = Enrichment	Teacher C = Enrichment	Teacher C = Intervention

By implementing this rotation cycle or something similar, each teacher will have a designated time for intervention with students who need extra help to complete assignments. A learning-focused classroom is not about the teacher covering the content but about the students learning the skills and knowledge from the prioritized standards. This happens when each student is accountable for the tasks that must be completed in order to demonstrate proficiency.

Converting Scores to Letter Grades

Many schools are accustomed or required to use percentages or letter grades to report students' scores. Although it is not impossible to use standards-based grading in conjunction with a percentage or letter grade system, there are some important issues to note. First of all, the scale used to calculate letter grades from a 100-point scale may be inconsistent from district to district or school to school. For example, one school uses the following conversion scale:

> 90–100 = A
>
> 80–89 = B
>
> 70–79 = C
>
> 60–69 = D
>
> 59 and below = F

But a school down the road uses a different scale, like the following:

> 93–100 = A
>
> 85–92 = B
>
> 77–84 = C
>
> 69–76 = D
>
> 68 and below = F

Therefore, grades between schools and districts may vary widely if letter grades based on a 100-point scale are used. If schools are intent on using these, they should at least agree on which type of conversion scale to use.

Another important item to consider is how to convert a proficiency scale score to a percentage score or letter grade, such as the following (Marzano, 2010):

3.75–4.00 = A+ 2.84–2.99 = B+ 2.34–2.49 = C+ 1.76–1.99 = D+ Below 1.00 = F

3.26–3.74 = A   2.67–2.83 = B   2.17–2.33 = C   1.26–1.75 = D

3.00–3.25 = A-   2.50–2.66 = B-   2.00–2.16 = C-   1.00–1.25 = D-

The conversion displayed in the previous list is one option for how a letter or percentage grade can be determined based on proficiency scale scores. If a school does not use plus or minus grades (such as A+ or A-), a simplified conversion scale could be used, such as the following (Marzano, 2010):

> 3.00–4.00 = A
>
> 2.50–2.99 = B
>
> 2.00–2.49 = C
>
> 1.00–1.99 = D
>
> Below 1.00 = F

In these conversions, a low A is the cut score for proficient. The rationale for this is that student performance at this level is at the expected or anticipated level—hence, the assignment of an A. Correlating a letter grade of A to 3.0 is recommended because the 3.0 level on every scale is a clear description of the prioritized standard. Marzano (2010) explained:

> The A begins at 3.0 because a score of 3.0 indicates that a student has demonstrated understanding of all content in a target learning goal with no major errors or omissions. This makes some intuitive sense—if a student's average score indicates that he or she knows everything that was taught for the target learning goals, he or she should receive an A. (p. 106)

The goal of educators is to have all students reach proficiency; thus, proficient students should earn an A. In the following story, a teacher shares differences he noticed when he helped his students focus on learning instead of point grabbing.

When Jeff Flygare aligned his students' grades with his proficiency scales, he saw a change in student attitudes. Rather than having students come in to discuss ways to get more points before the end of the semester, his students began to ask, "How do I become a better writer?" and "How do I analyze literature better?" The key difference between these comments and the previous point grabbing was that students were clear about their strengths and weaknesses. Because their grades were directly tied to a proficiency scale, they knew what they needed to do to get better. Instead of doing extra credit to enhance their average score for the semester, students became interested in demonstrating higher levels of proficiency on the prioritized standards.

Separating Knowledge and Behavior

As noted previously, in traditional grading systems, nonacademic skills such as effort, attendance, participation, punctuality, and ability to meet deadlines are typically incorporated into academic grades. For example, a teacher might tell students that 5 or 10 percent of their final grade will be based on their attendance and participation in class.

Secondary teachers, more so than primary teachers (Guskey, 2009a), tend to use several major projects or exams to compute a grade in addition to combining nonacademic factors with academic ones, such as averaging scores for each of the following items:

Attendance	Homework quality	Punctuality of assignment submissions
Class behavior or attitude	Journal entries	
Class participation	Laboratory projects	Reports or projects
Class quizzes	Major exams	Student portfolios
Classroom observations	Oral presentations	Work habits and neatness
Homework completion		

Guskey (2009a) found the following:

> Secondary teachers based their grading practices on what they per-
> ceived would best prepare students for college or the work world,
> believed that grades helped teachers influence students' effort and
> behavior, and were committed to the mathematic precision of grade
> calculations. (p. 1)

Some secondary teachers based grades on as few as two or three elements, while others incorporated evidence from as many as fifteen or sixteen (Guskey, 2006). Tony Winger (2005) summarized the effects of these practices on students:

> We had trained them to see grades as a commodity rather than as
> a reflection of learning. Comments from a student panel that my
> school district organized to investigate grading practices further elu-
> cidated the problem. Students reported that they see their school-
> work as a game they play for grades—a game that at best treats
> learning as incidental, and at worst distracts students from making
> meaning. One student referred to this grade game as academic buli-
> mia: Students stuff themselves with information only to regurgitate
> it for the test, with little opportunity for the thoughtful engagement
> that would produce deep understanding and growth. (p. 62)

When grades are not deliberately connected to learning, they provide little, if any, valuable feedback regarding students' academic strengths and weaknesses and can even be counterproductive. This system, like other traditional grading practices, is not compatible with standards-based grading. Winger (2009) explained how this can skew students' grades:

> When I began analyzing my grading practices several years ago, I
> was embarrassed by what I found. Although I claimed I wanted my
> students to think more critically and engage with the world more
> fully, my grading practices communicated a different message.
> Students received so much credit for completing work, meeting
> deadlines, and following through with responsibilities that these
> factors could lift a student's semester grade to a *B* or an *A*, even as
> other indicators suggested that the student had learned little. My
> grading practices communicated clearly that, despite my claims to
> the contrary, students' willingness and ability to comply mattered
> most. (p. 73)

Nonacademic factors should not be included when determining a student's academic performance grade, because the goal of the student's grade is to communicate how much he or she knows. Plus, there are many benefits to separating academic from nonacademic grades: parents appreciate the added level of specificity, and students become aware of what they need to work on. For teachers, using separate grades eliminates the need to compute a single grade that combines multiple facets of a student's performance. For example, a student can compensate for low understanding of the content and standards by maintaining perfect attendance, turning assignments in on time, and behaving appro-priately in class. A different student may understand content and standards perfectly well but receive a low grade because he or she is late to class, fails to turn assignments in on time, or acts inappropriately. Patricia Scriffiny (2008) said, "The system must not allow students to mask their level of understanding with their attendance, their level of effort, or other peripheral issues" (p. 72). The traditional practice of combining academic and nonacademic factors can inflate or deflate a student's grade, producing a number that means different things to different students, parents, and teachers.

The solution to this problem is to separate grades for achievement from those for homework, effort, work habits, behavior, and other nonacademic factors. Table 4.3 depicts one school district's version of a reporting form for nonacademic factors.

Table 4.3: Reporting Form for Nonacademic Factors

Factors	A Consistently exceeds expectations	B Consistently meets expectations	C Inconsistently meets expectations	U Does not meet expectations
Completes work **Turns work in punctually** **Is neat** **Makes up work**	Is punctual or early turning in assignments and goes beyond the stated requirements relative to neatness and adherence to conventions	Is punctual in turning in assignments and meets the stated requirements relative to neatness and adherence to conventions	Is not punctual in turning in assignments or does not meet the stated requirements relative to neatness and adherence to conventions	Is not punctual in turning in assignments and does not meet the stated requirements relative to neatness and adherence to conventions
Is prepared to learn **Arrives on time** **Has materials**	Always in class on time Brings needed materials to class and is always ready to work	Very few tardies Almost always brings needed materials to class and is ready to work	Some tardies Usually brings needed materials but sometimes needs reminders and redirection	Frequent tardies Often forgets materials and is rarely ready to get to work Often does not accept redirection
Participates in learning **Works well with others** **Shares ideas**	Routinely shares information or ideas when participating in discussions or groups A definite leader who contributes consistent effort	Usually shares information or ideas when participating in discussions or groups Often is a leader	Sometimes shares information or ideas when participating in discussions or groups Exhibits few instances of leadership Does the minimum required	Rarely shares ideas May refuse to participate In groups, relies on the work of others

Factors	A Consistently exceeds expectations	B Consistently meets expectations	C Inconsistently meets expectations	U Does not meet expectations
Follows classroom expectations **Stays on task** **Follows rules**	Consistently stays focused on the task and what needs to be done Very self-directed Always has a positive attitude	Focuses on the task and what needs to be done most of the time Works independently Often has a positive attitude	Focuses on the task and what needs to be done some of the time but needs to be reminded to keep on task Usually has a positive attitude	Rarely focuses on the task and what needs to be done Lets others do the work Needs reminders to perform classroom work Often has a negative attitude

Source: Adapted from Douglas County School District, 2003.

Fair and effective schools should assign grades that align with clear and consistent evidence of student performance (Wormeli, 2006). The following stories describe how two teams of educators changed their practices to more accurately report on both academic and nonacademic factors.

Michael Storrar's team decided to establish a new set of grading procedures that separated academic from nonacademic grades. In the new system, a student's grade was solely determined by his or her ability to demonstrate understanding of skills and concepts. For example, a student in a social studies class who did not finish a mapping assignment on time was encouraged to take it home, complete it, and turn it in the next day. In the old system, late work meant a deduction of ten points. However, Michael's team decided that if the map was completed correctly, the student would receive full credit. However, the student's grade for timeliness would be adjusted downward to account for the lateness of the assignment. Keeping the two grades separate ensured that they both retained their meaning.

Missy Mayfield's district separated academics from behavior by creating a common proficiency scale for life skills (behavior) that was posted in each classroom. Life skills and behavior scores were reported separately from academic grades. Some schools implemented Saturday school as a time for students to complete assignments. To celebrate excellent life skills performance, one school implemented Celebration Stations once a month for students achieving all 3s or 4s on life skills scales. Stations included culinary arts, Wii dance, iPad apps, jewelry making, and sports games, and students with the highest life skills scores got the first chance at their preferred activity. This was a significant change for many teachers, yet working through these issues and requiring consistency in practices helped students and parents better understand expectations.

Creating Meaningful Report Cards

The final step in designing a meaningful grading system is to create clear and meaningful methods to report students' scores and growth over time. In many schools, report cards are the main vehicle for communicating a student's grades and progress. Report cards can take many forms. Some are simply a one-page summary of a student's overall grades in the relevant subject areas. Others are electronic charts that summarize students' performance. While these can be effective, they are often not detailed enough to communicate to students and their parents exactly what students have done well and what they can continue to work on. When designing a standards-based system, it is important to consider the purpose of the report card and how best to convey achievement results.

A report card is first and foremost a communication tool. Guskey (2001) summarized three criteria that can be included on report cards:

> *Product criteria* relate to students' specific achievements or levels of performance. They describe what students know and are able to do at a particular point in time. Advocates of standards generally favor product criteria. . . . *Process criteria* relate not to the final results, but to how students got there. Educators who believe that product criteria do not provide a complete picture of student learning generally favor process criteria. . . . *Progress criteria* relate to how much students actually gain from their learning experiences. Other terms include learning gain, improvement grading, value-added grading, and educational growth. Teachers who use progress criteria typically look at how far students have come rather than where students are. (pp. 21–22)

The report card should be a valid representation of a student's progress and inform students and parents of strengths and challenges in learning the prioritized standards. The following three elements should be included on any report card. First, a report card should explain the prioritized standards that are important for each grade level or content area. Second, a report card should explain the proficiency-scale-based method used to assign grades. The report card might have an online link to the corresponding proficiency scales for the prioritized standards measured, or the proficiency scales could be an attachment to the report card. Third, a report card should report students' scores for the prioritized standards and their scores for life skills (such as work habits, attendance, and so on) separately.

These three elements can be included in many ways. The most important thing to consider when designing a report card is ease of interpretation. For example, the state of Kentucky's adoption of the Common Core included a redesign of its report card. Rather than long lists of standards for each subject area, the state created four to six clear and precisely worded *reporting standards* that expressed in parent-friendly language what students were expected to learn for that subject. Here, we provide several excerpts of report cards that could be used with a standards-based grading system.

Figure 4.1 shows a standards-based report card for ELA that separates academic performance from nonacademic performance. Students' academic scores are reported for three standards for Reading, five standards for Writing, and four standards for Speaking and Listening. Individual scores are reported for four life skills (that is, nonacademic areas): (1) participation, (2) work completion, (3) behavior, and (4) working in groups. The light-colored bars on each row of the report card indicate a student's final status for a particular measurement topic. The dark bars represent a student's initial status for each measurement topic. This system allows students and parents to see growth in addition to final scores.

Language Arts		0.0	0.5	1.0	1.5	2.0	2.5	3.0	3.5	4.0
Reading										
Word Recognition and Vocabulary	3.5									
Reading for Main Idea	2.5									
Literary Analysis	3.0									
Writing										
Language Conventions	4.0									
Organization and Focus	2.0									
Research and Technology	1.5									
Evaluation and Revision	2.5									
Writing Applications	1.0									
Speaking and Listening										
Comprehension	3.0									
Organization and Delivery	3.5									
Analysis and Evaluation of Media	2.0									
Speaking Applications	2.0									

Figure 4.1: Report card for ELA and life skills.

Continued on next page →

Life Skills		0.0	0.5	1.0	1.5	2.0	2.5	3.0	3.5	4.0
Participation	4.0									
Work Completion	3.0									
Behavior	4.0									
Working in Groups	2.5									

Source: Adapted from Marzano, 2010, pp. 115–117.

The report card excerpt in figure 4.2 illustrates a different way to report academic and nonacademic grades. Prioritized standards or key assignments are listed on the left with the student's academic scores for each item, while the student's nonacademic grade for timeliness in completing the assignment is listed on the right.

Social Studies			
Learning Target or Assignment		Life Skill (Timeliness)	
11.2.4 Civil War Battle Map	3.0	Late 1 day	2.0
11.5.6 Cause and Effect of War	2.5	On time	3.0

Figure 4.2: Report card excerpt for social studies.

This report card provides an extra level of specificity by reporting students' grades on individual assignments.

A more general example is shown in figure 4.3. Here, a student's overall academic scores are reported for language arts, math, science, social studies, and art on the left. On the right, overall nonacademic scores are reported for participation, work completion, behavior, and working in groups.

Language Arts	C (2.46)	Participation	A (3.40)
Mathematics	B (2.50)	Work Completion	B (2.90)
Science	C (2.20)	Behavior	A (3.40)
Social Studies	A (3.10)	Working in Groups	B (2.70)
Art	A (3.00)		

Figure 4.3: Report card for overall academic and nonacademic grades.

Report cards are usually common for all students in a school or district. Therefore, individual teachers may not be able to change report cards on their own. However, individual teachers can modify their gradebooks to reflect a standards-based grading perspective while they wait for school or district report cards to change. The following story explains how a teacher modified her grading practices by adjusting her gradebook.

Kristin Poage changed her gradebook headings from labels like *Homework*, *Classwork*, *Tests*, and *Quizzes* to standards-based headings such as *7.3.2 Writing Revision* and *10.4.3 Reading Comprehension*. First, this forced her to only give assignments and grades based on standards. Second, it made it easy for her to identify and target struggling students with interventions. With the previous headings, if a student failed to meet the target score in the area of *Homework*, Kristin had no information about what interventions would be most effective for that student. However, failure to meet the target for *7.3.2 Writing Revision* gave Kristin a clearer indication of what remediation and intervention was needed.

Summary

Educators need to align learning activities and assignments with proficiency scales and then give specific scores that reflect what a student understands or is able to do with the content. Separating academic and nonacademic grades is an important step toward authentic reporting of student achievement. Report cards, especially at the secondary level, may need to be redesigned to promote clear communication of what students are doing well and what they can still work on.

Grading Exceptional Learners

There is a small but distinct group of students in every school whose situation adds complexity to the grading process. Often referred to as *exceptional learners*, these students may need accommodations or modified instruction. In this chapter, we explain how to use proficiency scales to grade students classified as exceptional learners.

One might argue that all students are unique and exceptional learners. Students learn in a variety of different ways and have a variety of strengths and talents. However, the United States has defined several distinct groups as exceptional for the purposes of schooling and education. These include students with disabilities, English learners, and gifted and talented students. According to the Individuals With Disabilities Education Improvement Act of 2004, students with disabilities are those children "with mental retardation, hearing impairments (including deafness), speech or language impairments, visual impairments (including blindness), serious emotional disturbance . . . orthopedic impairments, autism, traumatic brain injury, other health impairments, or specific learning disabilities." English learners (ELs) are students who do not speak English as their primary language. These students may also be referred to as limited English proficiency (LEP) students or English as a Second Language (ESL) students (No Child Left Behind [NCLB], 2002). Students with disabilities and EL students will probably need extra help and support to attain 3.0 performance on the prioritized standards. On the other end of the spectrum, gifted and talented students are those who

> give evidence of high achievement capability in areas such as intellectual, creative, artistic, or leadership capacity, or in specific academic fields, and who need services or activities not ordinarily provided by the school in order to fully develop those capabilities. (NCLB, 2002, § 9101, para. 22)

It is important to address all three types of exceptional learners when assigning grades.

Giving fair and meaningful grades can be difficult when working with exceptional students. As Lee Ann Jung and Thomas Guskey (2010) explained:

> Assigning a failing grade to a student who has not met course or grade-level requirements because of a disability or difficulty with the language seems inherently unfair—especially if the student has worked hard, turned in assignments on time, and done what the teacher asked. (p. 31)

Well-developed proficiency scales can guide teachers' decisions regarding the level of support they need to provide exceptional students as well as how to grade them. Levels of support are closely associated with response to intervention (RTI), a system that provides differentiated instruction to meet the needs of all students so they achieve higher levels of academic and behavioral success (Campbell, Wang, & Algozzine, 2010; Kirk, Gallagher, Coleman, & Anastasiow, 2012; Mellard & Johnson, 2008).

A classroom will likely include students who fall in the three levels shown in figure 5.1. The majority of students will be able to use the general education proficiency scales (Hughes & Dexter, 2011). However, some students will require accommodations or modifications to be made to proficiency scales. *Accommodations* are supports put in place to help students achieve grade-level expectations. They do not change the level of the expectations for students, whereas modifications do. *Modifications* shift the expectations either up or down from the grade-level expectancies.

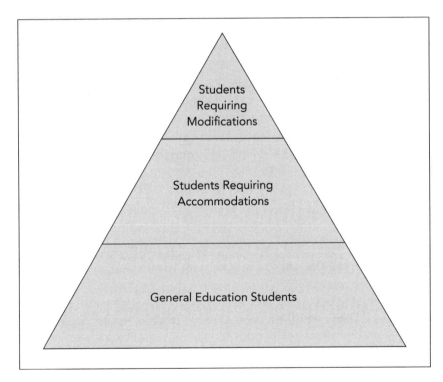

Figure 5.1: Levels of support.

To assign meaningful grades to exceptional students, teachers should create proficiency scales that incorporate accommodations or modifications. One way to identify students who may need accommodations or modifications is through preassessment, which informs teachers before instruction begins about where each student is in relation to the content. Each preassessment should be based on the proficiency scale being used in a course or grade level and should contain items for the 2.0, 3.0, and 4.0 levels of the scale. Since instruction for the content on a preassessment does not occur until after a preassessment is administered, it is likely that most students will fall short of the score 3.0 level. Students with disabilities and EL students may score even lower. Thus, these students will likely need extra support and scaffolding to achieve the 3.0 level. However, a gifted learner may score at the 3.0 level or higher, indicating that he or she should pursue more complex activities while the rest of the students experience the planned instruction.

After determining students' baselines, teachers are better equipped to create proficiency scales with modifications or accommodations to guide these differentiated learning experiences. To create such a proficiency scale, teachers should begin with the general education proficiency scale.

General Education Proficiency Scale

Table 5.1 (page 74) depicts a general education proficiency scale for seventh-grade ELA, based on the prioritized standard "The student will apply knowledge of organizational patterns found in informational text." The prioritized standard for all students is stated at score 3.0. The content at score 2.0 is simpler and is prerequisite to score 3.0 content. Pertinent vocabulary terms are also part of score 2.0. Score 4.0 involves performance beyond the learning goal. Notice that this scale contains both descriptors (described in chapter 2) and example activities (described in chapters 3 and 4) for the 2.0, 3.0, and 4.0 levels. Because the 1.0, 0.0, and half-point scores do not change from scale to scale, we do not include them with the scales in this chapter. The right side of the scale shows examples of how students can demonstrate their achievement of each level of the scale. It is important to understand that students could also demonstrate competency in other ways.

This proficiency scale is likely appropriate for the majority of seventh-grade students. However, there are times when students require accommodations or modifications. When this is the case, the general education proficiency scale should be changed to match these students' specific needs.

Table 5.1: Grade 7 ELA Scale for General Education Students

	Prioritized standard: The student will apply knowledge of organizational patterns found in informational text.	
4.0	In addition to score 3.0 performance, the student demonstrates in-depth inferences and applications that go beyond what was taught.	When the teacher provides the student with a folder containing an informational text cut into paragraphs, the student reads and organizes the text. The student then identifies the structure used by the author (for example, main idea with supporting detail, sequence, compare and contrast, fact and opinion) and cites specific examples within the text that are characteristic of the identified organizational structure.
		Given an informational text, the student discusses whether or not the author used the most effective organizational pattern and which other type of organization might enhance the text.
		The student writes an original text that incorporates a self-selected organizational structure.
3.0	The student will apply knowledge of organizational patterns found in informational text, such as: Sequence Cause and effect Compare and contrast Fact and opinion Description Proposition and support	When the teacher provides the student with a folder containing an informational text cut into paragraphs, the student reads and organizes the text and then identifies the structure used by the author (for example, main idea with supporting detail, sequence, compare and contrast, fact and opinion). The student classifies short selections of text using a graphic organizer.
2.0	The student will: Sequence three or more events in informational text Identify the cause and effect presented in a given text Identify what is being compared and contrasted in a given text Recognize or recall specific vocabulary, such as *sequence*, *cause*, *effect*, *compare*, *contrast*, *proposition*, and *support*	The student reads a text and highlights signal words within the text that indicate the structure of the text (for example, *first*, *second*, and *third* signal chronology; *because* or *as a result of* signal cause and effect; and *above*, *beneath*, and *beside* signal description). The student identifies different types of text and the type of organizational pattern often associated with the type of text (for example, biography often uses a sequence of events; editorials are often proposition and support). The student defines specific terms associated with organizational patterns.

Accommodations

Accommodations are changes to how information is presented, how students are asked to respond, where instruction takes place, and the timing or scheduling of instruction. Accommodations do not change the level of proficiency. Students who receive accommodations are still expected to achieve the same levels of proficiency as students without accommodations. Accommodations simply allow students to demonstrate their learning in the ways that work best for them. They do not result in lower or higher expectations and do not require a different grading system. It is important for teachers to document accommodations for specific students on the right side of a proficiency scale. Tables 5.2 (page 76), 5.3 (page 77), and 5.4 (page 79) illustrate how accommodations look on proficiency scales for students with disabilities, EL students, and gifted students, respectively.

Accommodations for Students With Disabilities

Students with disabilities normally receive accommodations during the instructional process on an as-needed basis. When this is the case, the scale should be adjusted to document the accommodations. The appropriate educators (for example, the classroom teacher, special education teacher, or multidisciplinary team) should collaborate to ensure that the example activities listed on the scale reflect the accommodations and supports the student typically receives during instruction. It is important to remember that these students are aiming for the same score 3.0 level as all general education students.

Scales that include accommodations are developed on a student-by-student basis, similar to an Individualized Education Program (IEP). Common examples of these accommodations include providing auditory supports (taped reading) or voice-to-text software; providing repetition and checks for clarity on a regular basis; seating the learner away from distractions; providing ongoing, specific feedback; allowing the learner to demonstrate understanding in a different mode (auditory versus written); providing additional time when necessary; providing a graphic organizer; and increasing the font size of printed text.

Educators should adjust the example activities in the right column of the scale to reflect the accommodations provided. The left side of table 5.2 is identical to the general education proficiency scale from table 5.1. However, the right side of the scale is personalized for a specific student with disabilities (accomodations are indicated in bold). It is important to note that the learning expectations for this student are the same as for the general education student.

Table 5.2: Grade 7 ELA Scale With Accommodations for Students With Disabilities

	Prioritized standard: The student will apply knowledge of organizational patterns found in informational text.	
4.0	In addition to score 3.0 performance, the student demonstrates in-depth inferences and applications that go beyond what was taught.	When the teacher provides the student with a folder containing an informational text (**of no more than four paragraphs**) cut into paragraphs, the student reads (**or listens to**) and organizes the text. The student then identifies (**from a list of possible structures**) the structure used by the author (for example, main idea with supporting detail, sequence, compare and contrast, fact and opinion) and cites specific examples within the text that are characteristic of the identified organizational structure. The student writes **or dictates** an original text that incorporates a self-selected organizational structure.
3.0	The student will apply knowledge of organizational patterns found in informational text, such as: Sequence Cause and effect Compare and contrast Fact and opinion Description Proposition and support	When the teacher provides the student with a folder containing an informational text (**of no more than three paragraphs**) cut into paragraphs, the student reads (**or listens to**) and organizes the text, then identifies (**from a list of possible structures**) the structure used by the author (for example, main idea with supporting detail, sequence, compare and contrast, fact and opinion). The student classifies short selections of text using a graphic organizer; **texts may be read to the student**.
2.0	The student will: Sequence three or more events in informational text Identify the cause and effect presented in a given text Identify what is being compared and contrasted in a given text Recognize or recall specific vocabulary, such as *sequence, cause, effect, compare, contrast, proposition*, and *support*	The student reads **or listens to** a text and highlights signal words within the text that indicate the structure of the text (for example, *first, second*, and *third* signal chronology; *because* and *as a result of* signal cause and effect; *above, beneath*, and *beside* signal description). The student identifies **three types of texts (for example, biography, article, or story)** and the organizational patterns usually associated with those types of texts. The student **matches terms** associated with organizational patterns **from a word bank to provided definitions**.

Accommodations for English Learners

Like those for students with disabilities, accommodations provided to EL students should be documented on students' individual proficiency scales. Common examples of these accommodations include showing examples of a completed assignment to model the correct format; writing assignments and directions on the board in both print and cursive; providing a bilingual assistant or interpreter to explain concepts in the students' primary language; providing manipulatives to help students complete certain tasks; rewriting story problems using short sentences, pictures, and illustrations to support understanding; teaching related vocabulary using pictures, visuals, and multimedia; providing reading materials at the instructional level of the student; providing audio recordings for the learner; providing adequate background information for the learner; and teaching reading strategies that enable ELs to predict, connect, question, and visualize a story.

As with students with disabilities, educators adjust only the right column of the proficiency scale to reflect the accommodations being provided; it is personalized to meet the EL student's specific instructional needs. Once again, the learning expectations are the same for EL students and general education students, but EL students have different ways to demonstrate their competence. Table 5.3 shows an example of the general education scale from table 5.1 (page 74) with accommodations for EL students (indicated in bold).

Table 5.3: Grade 7 ELA Scale With Accommodations for EL Students

	**Prioritized standard: The student will apply knowledge of organizational patterns found in informational text.**
4.0	In addition to score 3.0 performance, the student demonstrates in-depth inferences and applications that go beyond what was taught.	When the teacher provides the student with a folder containing an informational text (**of no more than four paragraphs**) cut into paragraphs, **and the text is read to the student or translated into the student's native language**, the student reads and organizes the text. The student then identifies the structure used by the author (for example, main idea with supporting detail, sequence, compare and contrast, fact and opinion) and cites specific examples within the text that are characteristic of the identified organizational structure. The student writes an original text **in his or her native language** that incorporates a self-selected structure.
3.0	The student will apply knowledge of organizational patterns found in informational text, such as: Sequence Cause and effect Compare and contrast Fact and opinion Description Proposition and support	When the teacher provides the student with a folder containing an informational text (**of no more than three paragraphs**) cut into paragraphs, **and the text is read to the student or translated into the student's native language**, the student organizes the text and identifies the structure used by the author (for example, main idea with supporting detail, sequence, compare and contrast, fact and opinion). The student classifies short selections of text **in his or her native language** using a graphic organizer; **the student may use a word-to-word dictionary, or texts may be read to the student**.

Continued on next page →

Prioritized standard: The student will apply knowledge of organizational patterns found in informational text.		
2.0	The student will: Sequence three or more events in informational text Identify the cause and effect presented in a given text Identify what is being compared and contrasted in a given text Recognize or recall specific vocabulary, such as *sequence, cause, effect, compare, contrast, proposition,* and *support*	**In his or her native language**, the student reads **or listens to** a text and highlights signal words within the text that indicate the structure of the text (for example, *first, second,* and *third* signal chronology; *because* and *as a result of* signal cause and effect; *above, beneath,* and *beside* signal description). **With the support of a translator**, the student identifies different types of text and the type of organizational pattern often associated with the type of text (for example, biography often uses a sequence of events; editorials are often proposition and support). The student **matches** terms associated with organizational patterns **from a word bank to provided definitions (presented pictorially or in the student's native language)**.

Accommodations for Gifted Learners

Like students with disabilities and EL students, gifted learners also require accommodations that should be documented on individual proficiency scales, as many may attain goals sooner than general education students. Accommodation activities for gifted learners include grouping them with other gifted students or higher-level learners; adjusting instruction to include advanced processes, products, and assessments; using thematic, project-based, and problem-based instruction to connect learning across the curriculum; allowing students to choose how to approach a problem or assignment; providing students the opportunity to design their own learning opportunities in areas of strength, interest, and passion; inviting students to explore different points of view on a topic of study and compare them; providing learning centers where students are in charge of their learning; asking students higher-level questions that foster critical thinking; requiring students to consider causes, experiences, and facts to draw a conclusion or make connections to other areas of learning; and employing a strategy wherein gifted students are allowed to demonstrate mastery of a concept right away rather than engaging in unnecessary skill practice. Teachers should also refrain from grouping gifted students with lower-level students for remediation purposes and from asking gifted learners to simply complete more work than other students.

Gifted students work toward the same prioritized standard as general education students, but the teacher personalizes the right column of each gifted student's scale by adjusting the description of the activity or raising the level of independence needed to perform tasks. Regardless of the methodology used to generate the activities, it is important to remember that the expectations (prioritized standards) are the same for all students. Table 5.4 shows a version of the general education proficiency scale from table 5.1 (page 74) that includes accommodations for gifted learners (indicated in bold).

Table 5.4: Grade 7 ELA Scale With Accommodations for Gifted Learners

	Prioritized standard: The student will apply knowledge of organizational patterns found in informational text.	
4.0	In addition to score 3.0 performance, the student demonstrates in-depth inferences and applications that go beyond what was taught.	When the teacher provides the student with a text, **the student reads it, identifies the structure** used by the author (for example, main idea with supporting detail, sequence, compare and contrast, fact and opinion), and cites specific examples within the text that are characteristic of the identified organizational structure. **The student then discusses the pros and cons of the author's use of that structure.** The student writes an original text that incorporates a self-selected organizational structure **and explains why the self-selected structure is effective.** **The student creates a student-generated task that demonstrates his or her understanding of organizational patterns found in informational texts.**
3.0	The student will apply knowledge of organizational patterns found in informational text, such as: Sequence Cause and effect Compare and contrast Fact and opinion Description Proposition and support	**The student rewrites a teacher-provided text using a different organizational structure. For example, when the teacher provides the student with an informational text that has a sequential structure, the student reads the text and rewrites it so the organizational structure is descriptive.** **When given a text, the student identifies the structure used by the author and suggests another organizational pattern that the author could have used to share the same information.**
2.0	The student will: Sequence three or more events in informational text Identify the cause and effect presented in a given text Identify what is being compared and contrasted in a given text Recognize or recall specific vocabulary, such as *sequence, cause, effect, compare, contrast, proposition,* and *support*	The student reads a text **and explains why certain words signal certain structures** (for example, *first, second,* and *third* signal chronology; *because* and *as a result of* signal cause and effect; *above, beneath,* and *beside* signal description). **The student writes a specific type of text (for example, a biography, article, or story), uses the organization pattern often associated with that type of text, and explains how it helped him or her organize the writing.** The student **lists and** defines specific terms associated with organizational patterns.

Modifications

In contrast to accommodations, modifications are changes to students' learning expectations. Modifications should only be made for a student whose IEP specifies such changes are necessary. For example, modifications for students with disabilities or EL students might include administering a lower-grade-level assessment, reducing the amount of content to be mastered, or reducing the difficulty and complexity of their prioritized standards. Modifications for gifted students can include having them complete higher-grade-level work or increasing the difficulty and complexity of their prioritized standards. When modifications are made for students, their grades show progress toward their *modified* prioritized standards, which are different from (simpler or more complex than) those of the general student population. The expectations are no longer the same. While modifications apply to only a small number of students, it is important for educators to understand that modifications change the descriptors on the left side of the scale (and therefore what students' grades mean) in addition to the example activities on the right side of the scale.

Modifications for Students With Disabilities

Creating a modified scale involves adjusting the prioritized standard at the 3.0 level and the simpler goal at the 2.0 level, as well as the example assessment activities for levels 2.0, 3.0, and 4.0. Sample modifications include shortening requirements or assignments and varying reading levels for independent reading. Some options for modifying scales for students with disabilities include moving the level descriptors up on the scale so that score 2.0 descriptors become score 3.0 descriptors and score 3.0 descriptors become score 4.0 descriptors, changing the example activities on the scale to make them simpler, and inserting descriptors from lower-grade-level scales.

Table 5.5 shows a scale modified for a student with disabilities, based on an IEP, in which the prioritized standard is less complex than the one for general education students. Notice that the general education prioritized standard states that students will *apply* knowledge of organizational patterns, whereas the modified standard states that the student will *identify* organizational patterns in a text. The levels of thinking on the modified scale are lower than the levels of thinking required by the same score level on the general education scale.

Table 5.5: Grade 7 ELA Scale With Modifications for Students With Disabilities

	General education prioritized standard: The student will apply knowledge of organizational patterns found in informational text.	
	Modified prioritized standard: The student will identify organizational patterns found in informational text.	
4.0	In addition to score 3.0 performance, the student demonstrates in-depth inferences and applications that go beyond what was taught.	The student identifies the sequence of events in an informational text. For example, after being read a text about the life of Abraham Lincoln, the student correctly restates the events in order.
		The student describes a cause-and-effect or compare-and-contrast pattern in an informational text.
		The student identifies statements that are fact and statements that are opinion. For example, given two sentences (such as *October is a month* versus *October is the best month*), the student correctly identifies which is a fact and which is an opinion.
3.0	The student will identify organizational patterns found in informational text, such as sequence, cause and effect, and compare and contrast.	The student identifies the sequence of events in an informational text. For example, after listening to a text about the life of Abraham Lincoln, the student correctly sequences pictures from the text. Or, after listening to a text about tornadoes, the student determines what happens after the air begins to rotate.
		The student identifies the cause and effect described in an informational text. For example, after listening to a text about smoking, the student states, "Smoking cigarettes can cause coughing, cancer, yellowing of teeth, and bad breath."
		The student identifies a compare-and-contrast organizational pattern. For example, a student can explain how a dog is like and unlike a cat after listening to the following sentences: "The dog, like a cat, makes a good pet. Unlike a cat, a dog likes to hide bones by burying them."
2.0	The student will: Sequence three or more events in informational text	When given a series of three pictures, the student identifies which one happened first, next, and last after listening to a story or informational text.
	Identify the cause of an event	After listening to a short informational text, the student identifies what happened first, next, and last.
	Identify a comparison in informational text	The student identifies the cause of an event based on a text. For example, "Icy roads are the cause of many automobile accidents."
	Recognize or recall specific terminology, such as *order*, *sequence*, *cause*, *compare*, and *alike*	The student identifies comparisons in an informational text, such as "Nebraska is a neighbor to South Dakota, Iowa, Kansas, and Colorado. Nebraska is larger than Iowa."

Modifications for English Learners

Like modifications for students with disabilities, modifications for ELs involve changing both the descriptors and the example assessment activities on the proficiency scale. Modifications for ELs include lowering the reading or difficulty level of texts, shortening assignments, using supplementary materials, allowing computer or word processor assistance, and modifying activities and assessments.

While EL students may require modified instruction and expectations for mastery, the ultimate goal for these students is to eventually reach the same score 3.0 level as all general education students. Consequently, we advise modifying scales for EL students by moving the prioritized standard to the 4.0 level. The 2.0 goal becomes the 3.0 goal, and new 2.0 expectations are created. This approach keeps the learning goal on the proficiency scale yet ensures the expectations for the learner are more appropriate for the individual student.

Table 5.6 shows a scale that has been modified for EL students. In order to support the student, some of the assessment activities ask the student to read or listen in his or her native language. However, the major difference between this scale and the general education scale is that the level of thinking on this scale is lower. This is represented in the type and length of text the student is asked to engage with.

Modifications for Gifted Learners

Modifications may also be necessary for gifted learners. These modifications might involve making learning goals more difficult; requiring students to apply their knowledge in unique, real-world situations; rephrasing prioritized standards as reflective guiding questions; and requiring students to create hypotheses, ask questions, and analyze their learning. Modified scales for gifted students increase the rigor and complexity of the expectations for each level of the scale. One way to do this is to shift the expectations downward: score 3.0 expectations become score 2.0 expectations, and score 4.0 expectations become score 3.0 expectations. Another way is to create a new, more complex 3.0 goal and adjust the 2.0 and 4.0 goals accordingly. Yet another method involves requiring gifted students to achieve 4.0 level expectations (rather than 3.0 level expectations). Example assessment tasks require students to extend their thinking through the development of products that demonstrate higher levels of thinking.

The proficiency scale in table 5.7 (page 84) has more complex expectations than the general education scale, as the expectations have been shifted.

Table 5.6: Grade 7 ELA Scale With Modifications for EL Students

General education prioritized standard: The student will apply knowledge of organizational patterns found in informational text.	
Modified prioritized standard: The student will apply knowledge of organizational patterns found in informational text.	
4.0 The student will apply knowledge of organizational patterns found in informational text, such as: Sequence Cause and effect Compare and contrast Fact and opinion Description Proposition and support	When the teacher provides the student with a folder containing an informational text (of no more than three paragraphs) cut into paragraphs, and the text is read to the student or translated into the student's native language, the student reads (or listens to) and organizes the text. The student then identifies the structure used by the author (for example, main idea with supporting detail, sequence, compare and contrast, fact and opinion). The student listens to a short informational text in his or her native language and draws pictures in a graphic organizer to represent key events. The student uses the pictures to retell the sequence of events in the text.
3.0 The student will: Sequence three or more events in informational text Identify the cause and effect presented in a given text Identify what is being compared and contrasted in a given text Recognize or recall specific vocabulary, such as *sequence, cause, effect, compare, contrast, proposition,* and *support*	The student listens to a short informational text in his or her native language and arranges pictures of events from the text in the order that they happened in the text. The student reads an adaptive text out loud to a teacher and highlights the signal words within the text that indicate the structure of the text (for example, *first, second,* and *third* signal chronology; *because* and *as a result of* signal cause and effect; *above, beneath,* and *beside* signal description). With the support of a translator, the student identifies different types of text and the type of organizational pattern often associated with the type of text (for example, biography often uses a sequence of events; editorials are often proposition and support). The student matches terms associated with organizational patterns from a word bank to provided definitions (presented pictorially or in the student's native language).
2.0 The student will: Identify the organizational pattern of sequence found in an informational text	The student listens to two short pieces of informational text. The teacher asks the student which piece of text uses the organizational pattern of sequence. The student identifies which text follows this pattern.

Table 5.7: Grade 7 ELA Scale With Modifications for Gifted Learners

General education prioritized standard: The student will apply knowledge of organizational patterns found in informational text.		
Modified prioritized standard: The student will compare and contrast the structures of texts and analyze their structures in detail to understand the role of particular sentences in developing and refining a key concept and to understand how each text's structure contributes to its meaning and style.		
4.0	In addition to score 3.0 performance, the student demonstrates in-depth inferences and applications that go beyond what was taught.	The student listens to a song (for example, "Scenes From an Italian Restaurant" by Billy Joel) and describes its structure using standard terminology (for example, use plot terminology such as *exposition*, *rising action*, *climax*, *falling action*, and *resolution* to describe the flashback in the Billy Joel song).
3.0	The student will: Compare and contrast the structure of two or more grade-appropriate texts and analyze how the differing structure of each text contributes to its meaning and style Analyze in detail the structure of a specific paragraph in a grade-appropriate text, including the role of particular sentences in developing and refining a key concept	The student compares and contrasts several texts (for example, "O Captain! My Captain!" by Walt Whitman or an excerpt from Russell Freedman's *Lincoln: A Photobiography* or Seymour Reit's *Behind Rebel Lines*) and then participates in a discussion where he or she explains the purpose and the value of the structures in the texts.
2.0	The student will: Recognize or recall specific vocabulary, such as *analyze*, *compare*, *concept*, *contrast*, *detail*, *develop*, *meaning*, *paragraph*, *refine*, *role*, *sentence*, *structure*, and *style* Describe the general structure of a specific paragraph in a grade-appropriate text Identify the general structure of a specific grade-appropriate text Recognize signal words or phrases associated with text structure (for example, *following*, *compared with*, *therefore*, *as a result of*) in a grade-appropriate text	The student reads a paragraph of informational text and then identifies and describes the organizational pattern used in the text. The student sorts words and phrases that signal text structures and explains what the structures communicate about how to read and understand the text.

Assigning Grades to Exceptional Students

To determine grades for exceptional students, teachers should follow the same guidelines described in chapter 4:

1. Examine the student's performance on assignments and assessments.

2. Give more weight to recent information (that is, information from later in the unit).

3. If necessary, discuss the content with the students to shed light on their learning progress.

4. Limit the use of zero.

However, teachers should use the exceptional student's individualized proficiency scale. For example, a teacher assigning a grade to a student with disabilities would assign scores to students based on how closely their performance matches the levels and descriptors on their unique proficiency scales. The following story discusses a teacher who modified proficiency scales for gifted students.

When she was the director of special programming for Douglas County School District in Castle Rock, Colorado, Robin Carey observed one of the teachers in her district implementing standards-based grading with her gifted learners. In past years, Ms. Sanders had been required to use the general education report cards for students in her fifth-grade gifted education class. This usually meant that her students received all As or all marks of 4.0, with an asterisk signifying they were working above grade level.

Ms. Sanders was concerned that this type of reporting was somewhat inexact. Obviously students were exceeding expectations, but by how much? The system didn't allow her to give students meaningful grades that showed what they were doing well and what they needed to work on. To remedy the situation, Ms. Sanders worked with other teachers of gifted learners, curriculum and assessment specialists, and administrators to devise a system that would be a more meaningful communication tool for gifted learners and their parents. Since most of her students were working at the sixth- and seventh-grade levels, Ms. Sanders used proficiency scales from those grade levels to assign scores. Ms. Sanders explained the system to her fifth-grade students and their parents at the yearly Back to School Night, saying, "Students working on the seventh-grade standards in math will have the prioritized standards for that grade level printed directly on their report cards, even though they are in fifth grade. A student might receive a mark of 3.0*, with the 3.0

signifying appropriate progress on the standards listed and the asterisk signaling standards that are higher than the fifth-grade level. The grade level of their standards will be indicated in the comments section of the report card."

On the report card, parents saw the targets for seventh-grade math and were able to ascertain where their child was on a continuum from 1.0 to 4.0 on those targets as the school year progressed. The connection between a student's progress on the learning targets in the classroom and the reporting system was now a match.

Summary

Grading practices for exceptional students can be capricious and unfair. Teachers, students, and parents cannot always be sure that grades accurately reflect student learning. In order to address this issue, schools can put into place a system of clear prioritized standards organized into proficiency scales that articulate competencies and example activities at each level. Students who perform at the 3.0 level have mastered the content. In the case of exceptional students, the regular scales can be adapted to reflect their educational needs. Using proficiency scales with accommodations or modifications can create a fair and consistent grading system that meets the needs of all students, including those with disabilities, EL students, and gifted learners. The next chapter presents strategies leaders can use to ensure a seamless and successful transition from traditional grading systems to standards-based grading.

Leadership

For many schools and districts, implementing the ideas outlined in this book may require substantive changes to their current systems, practices, and beliefs. Because such substantive changes are required, the transition to standards-based grading presents a unique set of challenges to school and district leaders. Linda Stevens described those challenges:

> This is not a task for the faint of heart. . . . All reform on a districtwide scale is tough, but moving a system to true standards-based grading is extraordinarily tough, long-term work and requires district leadership to tenaciously do the right thing for students. Waging war against the status quo requires the willingness to tackle layer after layer of difficulties in order to lead the way to new and purposeful assessment and grading practice. (personal communication, September 14, 2012)

Although the role of leaders and administrators has been addressed throughout this book, this chapter focuses on special considerations that will help leaders implement standards-based grading in their districts and schools. First we discuss planning for change, and then we lay out four years of implementation.

Planning for Change

Transitioning to standards-based grading is a systemic change and must be handled strategically and collaboratively within a school or district. Michael Fullan (2008) explained the magnitude of this type of initiative: "For organizational or systemic change, you actually have to motivate hordes of people to do something" (p. 63). DuFour and Marzano (2011) agreed: "No single person can unilaterally bring about substantive change in an organization. . . . Effective leaders recognize that they cannot accomplish great things alone" (pp. 1–2). Motivating and moving a school or district toward standards-based grading requires a strong, committed leader with a long-term vision and a detailed plan that allows all stakeholders to collaborate toward a final goal: a grading and reporting system that clearly communicates what students know and are able to do.

Unfortunately, time and resource constraints can prevent well-intentioned leaders from accomplishing the transition to standards-based grading. Thomas Guskey, Gerry Swan, and LeeAnn Jung (2011) explained, "Although school leaders would undoubtedly like to align their reporting procedures with the same standards and assessments that guide instructional programs, most lack the time and resources to do so" (p. 53). Additionally, leaders may become sidetracked by relatively insignificant issues. Brookhart (2011) cautioned that administrators may

> waste energy having hard discussions about details of grading practice that, by themselves, cannot accomplish real reform. Merely tweaking the details of a grading system can result in a system that makes even less sense than the one it was intended to replace. (p. 12)

In order to prevent debates about peripheral issues or wasted time and resources, school and district leaders should carefully plan each step they will take on the road to standards-based grading. Although school leaders may choose shorter or longer timelines for implementation, we recommend a four-year implementation plan. The sample four-year plan in table 6.1 outlines essential components of implementing a standards-based grading system.

Table 6.1: Sample Four-Year Standards-Based Grading Implementation Plan

Year One: Curriculum and Communication	Year Two: Capacity Building	Year Three: Implementation	Year Four: Continuation
Identify prioritized standards. Create (or revise) proficiency scales. Create (or revise) quality classroom assessments. Develop a communication plan.	Assemble a guiding team. Uncover current beliefs and attitudes about grading. Establish a group of "scouts" to explore the changes being made and report back. Enlist consultants. Educate the board of education.	Announce implementation. Implement new report cards. Encourage small-group experimentation. Organize book studies. Conduct school visits. Establish core beliefs. Involve parents. Involve technology staff.	Implement new teacher development.

Leaders should keep in mind that the components outlined in table 6.1 and detailed in this chapter may not be applicable for every school or district. Leaders may decide to accelerate or decelerate specific components or move them forward or back a year based on their school or district's individual needs. For example, Burkburnett School District in Burkburnett, Texas, designed a customized implementation plan for the transition to standards-based grading, shown in table 6.2.

Table 6.2: Burkburnett School District Standards-Based Grading and Assessment Four-Year Implementation Plan

	2011–2012	2012–2013	2013–2014	2014–2015
Common Understanding and Buy-In	Establish and train the guiding team. Implement districtwide professional development with consultant. Draft preliminary standards-based grading talking points and FAQs. Begin parent and community communication and high-er-ed connections.	Create universal understanding of proficiency scales. Revise common vocabulary and talking points. Produce a staff, parent, and community video about standards-based grading. Using surveys, measure the buy-in, levels of use, and concerns, and provide interventions. Collect feedback from staff through surveys, meetings, and conferences.	Implement targeted parent communication efforts. Implement standards-based report card during spring semester. Collect feedback about new report cards from teachers, parents, and students.	Continue collecting feed-back about new report cards throughout the year.
Prioritized Standards, Proficiency Scales, and Assessments	Begin writing proficiency scales. Begin creating common assessments.	Finish writing proficiency scales for all content areas, courses, and grade levels. Establish and begin implementation of a peer-review process for teacher-created documents. Implement professional development on next steps in standards-based grading with consultants.	Continue revising proficiency scales and assessment items through a peer-review process. Establish district benchmarks for each proficiency scale.	Continue revising proficiency scales and assessment items through a peer-review process. Implement district benchmarks.

Continued on next page →

	2011–2012	2012–2013	2013–2014	2014–2015
Integration With Existing Resources	Assess how standards-based grading fits with existing resources, electronic gradebooks, and expectations of professional learning teams.	Integrate standards-based grading into existing resources. Implement professional development on resources for standards-based grading.	Analyze revised math standards and align scales for K–8 implementation in 2014–2015.	Pilot and revise K–8 math scales. Analyze revised math scales and align scales for implementation in grades 9–12 in 2015–2016.
Teacher Portfolio of Evidence		Build portfolios that highlight scale and assessment creation and standards-based grading experiences. Identify prioritized standards. Write proficiency scales. Align and create assessments or benchmarks. Provide evidence of students tracking their own learning.	Continue portfolio development as administrators meet with teachers.	Continue portfolio development as administrators meet with teachers.
Homework Policy		Address issues for low-socioeconomic-status students and students without support. Create campus improvement teams to write homework guidelines for teachers (with guiding team members). Differentiate homework load based on proficiency level to motivate students. Distribute homework load by content.	Implement campus homework policies and revise as needed.	Implement campus homework policies and revise as needed.

	2011–2012	2012–2013	2013–2014	2014–2015
Student Evaluation and Goal Setting	Implement student-led conferences. Use student-friendly scales and have students self-track their learning. Provide feedback to parents after student-led conferences.	Continue support of student-led conferences, student-friendly scales, self-tracking of learning, and feedback to parents after student-led conferences.	Continue support of student-led conferences, student-friendly scales, self-tracking of learning, and feedback to parents after student-led conferences.	Continue support of student-led conferences, student-friendly scales, self-tracking of learning, and feedback to parents after student-led conferences.
Report Cards	Revise kindergarten report card to be used in 2012–2013.	Revise report card for grades 1–8 to be used in 2013–2014. Implement new kindergarten report card. Create proficiency scales for life skills.	Pilot new report card for grades 1–8. Revise high school report card to be used in 2014–2015.	Implement new report card for grades 1–8. Pilot new high school report card.
Administrator Development	Meet with consultants. Attend assessment conference.	Meet with consultant via email and webinar. Form online networking group. Begin book study. Conduct site visits to schools with standards-based grading in place.		

Source: Adapted from Burkburnett Independent School District, 2012a.

Table 6.2 (page 89) illustrates the idea that school and district leaders should feel free to personalize and adapt the sample plan from table 6.1 (page 88) to meet their school or district's individual needs. Regardless, administrators need to understand each element in each year in order to facilitate a clean implementation.

Year One: Curriculum and Communication

Standards prioritization, proficiency scale, and assessment work should take place during year one. However, beginning that work does not mean an administrator must formally announce the transition to standards-based grading. Waiting until year two or three to formally announce the official implementation of standards-based grading often allows an administrator to build a foundation of solid proficiency scales and assessments before asking teachers to commit to a new system of grading. Also, waiting to announce the transition can help administrators avoid unnecessary resistance that sometimes arises from teachers, parents, or staff members who are simply uninformed or who lack a clear understanding of standards-based grading.

We recommend that administrators spend the first year leading curriculum work with standards, scales, and assessments to form a foundation that will make the official transition to standards-based grading much easier when it is announced. The following story describes how one of the authors used this delayed announcement strategy to facilitate change in her Colorado district.

> When she was the director of curriculum, instruction, and assessment for Douglas County School District in Colorado, Tammy Heflebower realized that the district lacked a clearly articulated K–12 curriculum, a weakness that could prevent a smooth transition to standards-based grading. Consequently, she and her team led curriculum work, such as identifying prioritized standards, creating proficiency scales, and writing common assessments, before announcing the transition to standards-based grading. This strong foundation created a body of shared knowledge and experiences that helped all stakeholders understand and embrace the changes to grading and reporting systems once they were implemented.

Waiting to officially announce standards-based grading, however, does not mean that an administrator should refrain from talking about it with staff, students, and parents. In fact, year one is a critical time for administrators to begin putting structures in place that will help them communicate with stakeholders throughout the standards-based grading implementation process.

Strategic communication during the transition to standards-based grading is one of the primary responsibilities of school leaders. Miscommunication between individuals is unfortunate, but when it occurs on a larger scale, fixes are more difficult and the stakes are much higher. Rather than do damage control or try to pick up the pieces after a large-scale miscommunication, it is critical to invest time in clear, consistent communication at the front end of implementation. A purposeful communication plan maximizes the chances that stakeholders will support the change.

When developing a communication plan, leaders should consider how many people will hear, see, or read each message. They must also customize each message for the target stakeholder group and ensure that each group has multiple opportunities to learn about standards-based grading. To accomplish this, leaders should begin with three key aspects of communication: (1) clearly defined goals and desired outcomes; (2) understanding of situational challenges, resources, and allies; and (3) sensitivity toward stakeholder audiences, including allies, skeptics, and vocal dissenters. Table 6.3 contains guiding questions leaders should consider as they plan for each of these aspects of communication.

Table 6.3: Communication Considerations

Clearly defined goals and desired outcomes	What are you trying to accomplish?
	What is success going to look like?
	How will you measure success?
	Are you simply hoping for support of new grading practices, or are you hoping for enthusiastic applause?
	Is your effort part of a pilot during which you will want stakeholders to give feedback and possibly testimonials?
Understanding of situational challenges, resources, and allies	How do you and your efforts fit into the bigger picture?
	Are you leading this initiative for the school or for the district?
	Generally, are people in favor of this, or are they against it? Do they even know about it? What do they know about it?
	What other recent change initiatives have been successful or have failed? Why? How closely were they related to your changes in grading practices?
	What resources are available to you?
	How much time do you have? How much time do you need?
	Who else could help? How much time do they have?
	Who are likely to be the biggest supporters of this change initiative? Why?
	Are there others who would be supportive and offer help if they knew more about what was going on?
Sensitivity toward stakeholder audiences, which include allies, skeptics, and vocal dissenters	What other stakeholder groups influence the success of your standards-based grading efforts?
	Who are they, and what motivates them?
	What do you hope to achieve with each of these groups?

As the plan is developed, leaders need to think about the different communication channels currently in place and how each could be used with their stakeholders.

Selecting the appropriate medium for each message is another important aspect of creating a communication plan. The communication matrix in figure 6.1 can help leaders decide which type of communication to use. Face-to-face communication is the first medium listed, and we have evaluated the criteria as an example. The first criterion, *impact*, can be very high in face-to-face communication. *Immediacy* can vary in face-to-face communication, but a high amount of *time and effort* are required, especially when the change is significant. Finally, *interactivity* can be very high during face-to-face communication.

	Impact	Immediacy	Time and Effort	Interactivity
Face to face	High	Variable	High	High
Email				
Handouts or print				
Internet				
Video				
Other				
Other				

Figure 6.1: Communication matrix.

Leaders should carefully consider the four criteria for all communication media and seek to find a balance of methods to reach as many stakeholders as possible. For example, Principal A may not be able to have a parent meeting for three weeks, which would make the immediacy (and likely the impact) of face-to-face communication much lower than for Principal B, who already has one scheduled for this Thursday evening.

Finally, remember that effective communication is genuine and even spontaneous. When done well, what is written and delivered about a change aligns with the key message and desired outcomes of the initiative. To achieve this communicative consistency, different versions of the standards-based grading message should be thoughtfully developed. One approach to accomplish this is to develop an elevator speech, a cab-ride speech, and a stuck-in-the-airport speech.

Elevator Speech

The elevator speech is a familiar concept to many. It is often employed by lobbyists who know they may not have many opportunities for lengthy one-on-one conversations with busy senators or representatives but rather brief chances—say, on an elevator—to sway legislators to vote a particular way on an issue. A leader might use an elevator speech with a service club member who asks about standards-based grading or when he or she is stopped in the grocery store or another nonschool setting. Although the purpose is different, the process of creating an elevator speech distills a message down to its most important elements. The following is an example of an elevator speech for standards-based grading:

> As you may know, the role of our staff is to educate all students to proficient levels. In order to do so, we are revising our grading practices to be aligned to the standards students must meet. That way, grades will be a clearer indication of what students have learned, not simply a measure of how much work they can turn in or how hard they might try in class. Learning is the indicator of success.

Communicating a clear yet succinct message is critical. In an elevator speech, the goal is to deliver a strong, simple, and short message.

Cab-Ride Speech

Sometimes, leaders have lengthier opportunities to deliver their message. In those cases, more detail can be included to help listeners understand standards-based grading in more depth. Cab-ride speeches are particularly useful in these situations. A cab-ride speech has more details than an elevator speech and includes an example or detail for each key point. A cab-ride speech would add the following information to the foundation laid by an elevator speech:

> Our new state standards require that students be competent at higher levels in fewer things and understand concepts more deeply. One way to help teachers better understand and prioritize these standards is to create proficiency scales. These proficiency scales clearly articulate what students are to know and to what degree, so teachers can more accurately and reliably monitor student progress. After scales are in place, we can align classroom assessments and grading practices to ensure that the grades students receive are indicative of how well they have learned the important standards.

In a cab-ride speech, a leader has a bit more time to describe the situation and the rationale. Adding some specificity helps assuage listeners' concerns and address their objections.

Stuck-in-the-Airport Speech

Finally, leaders should be prepared to deliver a speech that fully develops the reasons for moving to standards-based grading. The stuck-in-the-airport speech explains the reasons for the change with several examples and illustrations for each point. For example:

> Do you remember a time when you didn't have to study at all in a class and you got a high grade? Or, conversely, a time when you worked super hard and learned what the teacher said was important, only to find out that the questions on the test didn't match that at all? This often happens, and it indicates a misaligned grading

system. In order to correct the problem, a system needs to ensure that grades are fair, reliable, and motivational for students. We have some ways to help with that. What do you think would motivate a student to study for an exam? We have found that feeling tricked when taking an exam (studying one thing and being assessed on something different) is really discouraging for students. What if all students could clearly articulate what they needed to know and do to be successful in any given class? What if they knew what steps to take to increase their own learning? What if they knew they would have multiple opportunities to understand what was important and early attempts wouldn't be held against them? Those are some of the components of a standards-based system.

In a standards-based system, learning essential content is the expectation for all students, and how long that takes or when it occurs is more flexible than it was in the past. Life skills are also very important in a standards-based system. In fact, they are so important they get their own grade. Students in standards-based systems get clear feedback about progress they are making on their knowledge and skills, as well as their behaviors and growth, and they track their own progress as well.

In order to make this type of system a reality, foundational components are necessary. For instance, teachers must collaborate and agree on prioritized standards to teach for every course and every grade level. After doing that, they work together to create proficiency scales that clearly articulate how to be successful with the prioritized standards. These scales are shared with students and parents, so there are no surprises about what success looks like or where a student is on his or her learning journey toward proficiency. After that, teachers need to be sure the assessments are aligned to these scales, which ensures that what is taught is actually measured to the degree of understanding required by the standard. It keeps students more motivated, because assessment becomes a natural part of the learning process rather than a stressful experience tacked onto the end. Teachers must also be sure there is strong alignment to the instructional activities that will help students deeply understand and use the knowledge and skills. This means no more busywork or activities that have no relevance to true comprehension and more deep discussions about how the learning is applied in the real world.

This also means that when you receive grades as a student or you see them as a parent, you know they are directly derived from an understanding of the content and processes, not inflated by meaningless bonus points unrelated to learning. All of this means significant changes to our current beliefs and practices. Just as doctors learn new and less invasive techniques for surgery on a regular basis or use new tests to provide more detailed analyses of a patient's health, so too must educators learn new ways to ensure all students learn important knowledge and skills. How we report student achievement must directly relate to what students know and can do.

> We know these changes will take time, energy, new thinking, and some experimentation in order to get it right. We ask for your help and support through this journey.

The airport speech has more details about the changes and the reasons for them. It also contains some analogies and questions for the audience to ponder. As illustrated in these examples, the curriculum and communication work that takes place during year one lays the foundation for successful implementation of standards-based grading.

Year Two: Capacity Building

During year two, administrators build capacity about the fundamental aspects and processes of standards-based grading. An administrator's capacity involves awareness of his or her school or district's strengths and an understanding of obstacles that might inhibit improvement efforts. Fullan (2008) defined capacity building as follows:

> Capacity building concerns competencies, resources, and motivation. Individuals and groups are high in capacity if they possess and continue to develop knowledge and skills, if they attract and use resources (time, ideas, expertise, money) wisely, and if they are committed to putting in the energy to get important things done *collectively* and *continuously*. (p. 57)

As leaders prepare to implement standards-based grading in their school or district, it is important that each person leading the change develop a well-rounded understanding of grading practices. Joanne Rooney (2008) observed that "principals expect teachers and students to take ownership of their own learning. They must expect no less of themselves as they continually seek to improve their professional knowledge and skills" (p. 82). Rooney (2008) advised leaders:

> Become informed about any programs your school is considering adopting or has initiated. Research them thoroughly and insist that teachers do the same. Avoid the pitfall of adopting silver bullets of education reform. Easily accessible online resources provide extensive information about any creditable program. (p. 82)

One way for principals and district leaders to cultivate their own knowledge while expanding their staff's awareness is to seek out and distribute information about standards-based grading. They could share a standards-based grading article (or excerpt from an article) with the staff each month. Leaders should also consider attending conferences, reading online blogs, and engaging in discussions with leadership groups from schools or districts that are also implementing standards-based grading.

While administrator learning is an important part of capacity building, systemic changes require other stakeholders to learn too. Thomas Hoerr (2007) stated, "Although today's principals have neither the time nor the expertise to be the instructional leader in the traditional sense—by knowing the most—we can exercise instructional leadership just as powerfully through facilitating teachers' learning" (p. 84). Michael Barber and Mona Mourshed (2007) concluded that "the quality of an education system cannot exceed the quality of its teachers" (p. 16). Therefore, the key priority during year two is to build capacity, knowledge, and understanding in key stakeholders such as teachers, students, and parents.

Burkburnett School District created a document to clearly articulate the process for building capacity, including the responsibilities of administrators at the district level as well as teachers and administrators at the school level, as shown in table 6.4.

Table 6.4: Standards-Based Grading and Assessment Capacity Building and Focus Activities for Burkburnett School District

District Efforts	
Monthly Newsletter	November: Separating academics from behavior
	December: Prioritizing standards
	January: Writing quality proficiency scales
	February: Busting the myths of standards-based grading
	March: Aligning assessments to scales
	April: Honoring most recent learning
	May: Rechallenging and redoing
Webinars	November: Administrative teams
	January: All district staff
	May: Guiding teams
Book Study	Administrators: *The Principal as Assessment Leader* (Guskey, 2009b)
	Certified staff: *The Teacher as Assessment Leader* (Guskey, 2009c)
Family and Community Activities	Monthly newspaper article
	Brief student and staff videos for district website and board of education meetings
School Efforts	
Faculty Activities	Monthly trainings on focus topics led by guiding teams using common presentations and activities
Professional Learning Team (PLT) Discussion	Guiding questions from *The Teacher as Assessment Leader*

Source: Adapted from Burkburnett Independent School District, 2012b.

As seen in table 6.4, Burkburnett leaders used newsletters, webinars, book studies, family and community activities, faculty activities, and professional learning team (PLT) discussions to facilitate deeper understanding and the implementation of standards-based grading in their district.

During year two, as in year one, administrators may choose to build capacity before they formally or officially announce a transition to standards-based grading. There are five specific activities that leaders can engage in to build capacity: (1) assembling a guiding team, (2) uncovering current beliefs and attitudes about grading, (3) establishing a group of scouts, (4) enlisting consultants, and (5) educating the board of education.

Assemble a Guiding Team

Assembling a dedicated, knowledgeable, and enthusiastic guiding team is a crucial element of implementing standards-based grading in a school or district. John Kotter and Holger Rathgeber (2005) advised leaders to "make sure there is a powerful group guiding the change—one with leadership skills, credibility, communications ability, authority, analytical skills, and a sense of urgency" (p. 130). A fairly common configuration for a guiding team consists of department chairpersons (or grade-level representatives in elementary situations), assistant principals, the principal, at least one counselor, and parents. In most cases, the size of a guiding team is directly proportional to the size of the district or school. The exact makeup is flexible but should take into account some representation from all areas of the school—including students. Each team should also include technology staff, since grading practices should drive technology rather than the other way around; their expertise and input will be especially valuable during years three and four.

Note that guiding team members may or may not be members of the teams that identified prioritized standards, created proficiency scales, or wrote assessments in year one. We recommend using an application process (separate from the application process described in chapter 2) to begin putting this guiding team together. As an example of how guiding team members can be identified, the application in figure 6.2 was used in Colorado's Douglas County School District to recruit members for their standards-based grading guiding team.

Dear applicants,

The purpose of the standards-based guiding team is to assist with district efforts toward a coherent plan to ensure all of our students receive fair, accurate, and reliable data about their progress in grade levels and courses. By involving representatives from many schools, the guiding team will have representative viewpoints and build on the work that has already been done.

Teachers who are interested in participating in this guiding team should complete the short application (below) and return it to the director of curriculum and instruction by May 8. We anticipate that the guiding team will consist of twenty-five members initially, from both elementary and secondary. Our primary consideration when selecting members will be content expertise and representation from all feeder systems and levels.

Figure 6.2: Guiding team application.   Continued on next page →

Application

Name: _____

Briefly describe your educational background and content-area expertise (for example, advanced degrees, additional training, and so on):

How do you determine grades for your students?

What information has influenced your grading practices?

What frustrations (if any) do you have with current grading practices?

If you are selected to participate on the standards-based guiding team, are you comfortable sharing information with other faculty and staff at your school and obtaining feedback from them? _____

Teacher Signature: _____

Principal Signature: _____

Source: Curriculum & Instruction Team 2006–2007, Douglas County School District. Used with permission.

As you assemble a guiding team, be aware that certain types of people are especially desirable for this team. In his book *The Tipping Point*, Malcolm Gladwell (2000) described how to identify key people who can cause an idea to grow quickly. Gladwell (2000) stated, "The success of any kind of social epidemic is heavily dependent on the involvement of people with a particular and rare set of social gifts" (p. 33). He specifically identified three types of people integral to any successful change process: (1) connectors, (2) mavens, and (3) salesmen.

Connectors are skillful at taking ideas and information from a specialized situation and translating them into messages that large groups of people can easily understand. They know many people from a variety of realms and enjoy connecting one group to another. They often say things like "I know someone you should talk to." As a leader, it is important to identify the connectors in your organization. Involve these people in discussions to give them details about standards-based grading, and then invite them to share what they learned with groups of parents, teachers, or students.

Another key group is the *mavens*. Gladwell (2000) described mavens as "information brokers, sharing and trading what they know" (p. 69). Mavens might be parents, teachers, or even students who love to know a lot about a specific topic and share that information in helpful ways. Mavens want to help others make informed decisions. They say things like "I was researching that last week and found . . ." or "Have you thought about adding this information to yours?" Find the mavens, help them understand why and how standards-based grading can solve problems in your school or district, and then ask them to use what they've learned to help others find solutions.

The final key group is *salesmen*. These persuasive and charismatic individuals are great negotiators with powerful people skills. They enjoy selling a message. Make sure that salesmen have a clear idea of what standards-based grading involves and how it can help teachers and parents meet the needs of students and support learning, and then ask them to help you build support for the idea.

In addition to selecting permanent members of the guiding team, we recommend implementing an open chair at guiding team meetings, which allows additional people to attend particular meetings. Any teacher can fill the open chair for his or her department, or a parent might fill the open chair. In fact, anyone curious about the process or about what goes on at guiding team meetings should be welcome to come and participate, which adds transparency to the process. Fullan (2008) commented on this type of transparency:

> By transparency I mean openness about results. I also mean openness about what practices are most strongly connected to successful outcomes. What is inside the black box of implementation? How can we help others learn about and understand the inner workings of implementation? (pp. 99–100)

Leaders can offer open chair spots on a first-come, first-served basis to all teachers in a department or school or can invite specific people they feel would benefit from the experience. Staff members who fill open chairs are included in the meeting with the same level of involvement as permanent members of the team and must abide by the norms previously established by the original team.

Uncover Current Beliefs and Attitudes About Grading

Assuming that people think or feel a specific way is not a productive strategy for implementing systemic change. When school or district leaders are interested in reforming their grading systems, it is extremely helpful for them to find out what teachers' current beliefs and attitudes about grading are. One way to find this information out is to ask questions that will spark grading-related conversations. For example, what does it mean if a student gets a 92 percent, or what specifically does a student know if he or she received a B on an exam? If grades are ever going to truly reflect learning and serve as dependable summaries of what students know and can do, school leaders must find out about existing grading philosophies and practices.

Surveys offer a formal method for collecting data about beliefs and attitudes toward grading. Figure 6.3 (page 102) shows a sample grading survey that may be used by a school to obtain baseline information about attitudes toward grading and grading practices.

Please respond to the following questions about grading. Candid responses are critical and honored as we work toward a common grading system.

What is the definition of a grade?

Why do we grade?

What should a grade represent?

What role should homework, attendance, behavior, and participation play in grading?

What role should retesting play in grading?

Is grading fair and equitable in your classes? Why?

Figure 6.3: Grading survey.

To facilitate the administration of surveys and compilation of results, leaders can use anonymous electronic survey tools such as SurveyMonkey (www.surveymonkey.com) or Zoomerang (www.zoomerang.com).

After all staff members have completed a survey, small groups of teachers can discuss survey answers to discover common beliefs and concerns about current grading practices. Data from a grading survey can be a starting point for guiding team conversations or discussions with parents. Data can also help leaders determine what types of professional development are most beneficial as implementation progresses.

Establish a Group of Scouts

In addition to assembling a guiding team, leaders may also want to establish a group of scouts. Scouts are staff members who explore the challenges ahead and investigate what is to come. Often, this involves visiting schools who have successfully implemented standards-based grading and reporting back about what they observed. Scouts do not necessarily need to be on the guiding team, but they do need to be carefully selected to represent various teacher groups in a school, including teachers who are ready for the change and those who are still on the fence. In fact, leaders may build more capacity in the initial stages by recruiting scouts from outside the guiding team whenever possible.

The criteria for selecting scouts should be their ability to collaborate successfully with each other as they investigate standards-based grading. Commonly, scouts attend a training or workshop to explore standards-based grading together. At the end of each training day, the scouts meet to reflect on what they learned and discuss key points. Upon returning from the training, the scouts debrief with the guiding team and, if appropriate, present their findings to the entire staff. If resources allow, schools should consider sending a second group of scouts to learn about the concept and bring back additional information. This is highly effective if a school is organized in professional learning communities but can be successful for any type of collaborative team structure the school may have in place. Scouts work within these collaborative groups to increase everyone's initial understanding of standards-based grading.

Enlist Consultants

During systemic changes, collective wisdom is critical, and investing in help from outside consultants can greatly assist in the learning curve and lend an additional layer of credibility to an initiative. While a guiding team and scouts will help build capacity within a staff, schools and districts sometimes need assistance and perspectives from external sources. Consultants are out-of-district experts who can ascertain existing practices and assist with long-term planning. Professional development can also be provided by consultants who bring fresh perspectives and new voices to grading conversations.

Consultants working directly with a school can serve as critical friends to administrators and teachers involved in the change. In this role, the consultant, or team of consultants, can bring clarity and address critical issues directly while not being a daily colleague of the teachers or principal. For example, the principal of a school might have a clear understanding of standards-based grading and be ready to implement large-scale changes. However, teachers might not yet be completely comfortable with the process, and therefore could become hostile toward the principal. By recognizing that the teachers and principal are not on the same page, a consultant could bridge the gap by helping the principal hear and respond to areas of difficulty for the teachers.

Consultants can also address old and ineffective, but popular, grading practices in a nonpersonal way and serve as a catalyst to help teachers suspend their traditional attitudes about grading. Getting a consultant involved early in the process also provides a valuable resource for the members of the guiding team as they develop their expertise to guide the rest of the school. Consultants can also train guiding team members to be in-house experts for the school or district later in the process.

Figure 6.4 (page 104) shows an example of the plan that Danielle Tormala created to involve a team of consultants in their standards-based grading implementation process.

Date	Workshop Description
8/30/11	**Formative Assessment and Standards-Based Grading Overview With Consultant 1** Discuss details of training and specific district needs Create an intranet site for interested teachers to communicate with other teachers at similar stages of standards-based grading Build interest in participating in a guiding team at schools
9/22/11	**Formative Assessment and Standards-Based Grading (High School Only) With Consultants 1 and 2** Address special concerns about standards-based grading at the high school level Explain how to overcome high school–level obstacles to standards-based grading Encourage more teachers to be a part of the intranet site Review and provide feedback on proficiency scales written by high school teams
12/2/11	**Background Knowledge and Vocabulary Development for Implementing Proficiency Scales With Consultant 3** Emphasize how to identify guaranteed vocabulary for students and where vocabulary fits into proficiency scales
6/5/12 & 6/6/12	**Development of Quality Common Assessments With Consultant 4** Emphasize how to use proficiency scales to create quality common assessments Address criteria for quality common assessments Create beginning assessments and review samples of previous assessments
7/12/12	**Common Core State Standards With Consultant 4** Infuse CCSS into proficiency scale and assessment work Connect standards-based grading components with CCSS instructional shifts
7/24/12	**Building and District Leadership Retreat With Consultant 1** Validate and direct leadership staff about areas of strength and challenges regarding standards-based grading and their school improvement efforts Build knowledge about standards-based grading components through question-and-answer sessions
Fall 2012	**Consultant Group Review of Proficiency Scales** Review proficiency scales and provide written and verbal feedback
9/26/12	**Board of Education Standards-Based Grading Workshop With Consultant 2** Formally train the board of education on key concepts of standards-based grading Personalize training with question-and-answer sessions

Date	Workshop Description
9/27/12	**Formative Assessment and Standards-Based Grading (Grades 7–12) With Consultant 2** Provide standards-based grading training to an additional cohort of secondary teachers
12/5/12	**21st Century Skills With Consultant 1** Connect 21st century instructional strategies and skills to components of standards-based grading Expand district vision to include additional instructional support for teachers
3/12/13	**Reflective Practice and Questioning With Consultant 1** Provide additional training about instructional components for successful standards-based grading implementation **21st Century Skills With Consultant 1** Repeat session for a new cohort of teachers
3/13/13	**Overview: Student Engagement, 21st Century Skills, and Reflective Practice With Consultant 1** Repeat session for a new cohort of teachers Train additional teachers in specialized standards-based grading instructional concepts **Reflective Practice and Questioning With Consultant 1** Repeat session for a new cohort of teachers
7/16/13	**Effective Supervision of Standards-Based Grading With Consultant 1** Align teacher evaluation systems with components of standards-based grading Personalize interactions through question-and-answer sessions
Fall 2013	**Webinar Series With Consultant 1 and Implementing Educators** Answer questions about implementation of standards-based grading

Source: Danielle Tormala. Used with permission.

Figure 6.4: Sample plan for involving consultants.

Many of the components of a standards-based system are integrated throughout the multiyear plan in figure 6.4, which also includes web conferences and electronic interactions.

Educate the Board of Education

When leaders want to implement changes to their school or district's grading policies, the board of education's support will be absolutely critical. However, it is important to give board members the information most useful to them. Too often, standards-based grading initiatives can be sidetracked by uninformed or misinformed board of education members or by overwhelming the board with unnecessary details about school-level implementation. Superintendents should ensure that board members have information about the impact of standards-based grading on parents, students, and teachers and the financial and budgetary considerations involved in the change. To help them understand the ideas behind standards-based grading, leaders can share journal articles and chapter excerpts with members. Update the board of education throughout the implementation process to ensure it knows what has been done and what is planned for the future. Many districts who have implemented standards-based grading have established a standing agenda item for it on the board's agenda. This gives them a consistent opportunity to share information, seek input, and answer questions.

Year Three: Implementation

During year three, administrators continue to build capacity for the transition to standards-based grading. However, during year three, capacity building extends beyond leaders and school staff members to groups who may not have been involved yet. Additionally, new members may be added to the guiding team in year three and fresh groups of scouts may be organized. New members and groups may include teachers who were previously unsure about the idea or were waiting to be invited to the initiative. Finally, year three is a good time to officially and formally announce the transition to standards-based grading. It is also the time to implement new report cards, encourage small-group experimentation, organize book studies, conduct school visits, establish core beliefs, involve parents, and involve technology staff.

Announce Implementation

By this point, administrators will have laid a strong foundation of curriculum work, effective communication, and capacity building. Announcing the transition to standards-based grading and reporting practices, therefore, will be much easier during this year than it might have been previously. It is likely that by this time, many teachers will already see the benefits of standards-based grading, and because the work of prioritizing standards, creating proficiency scales, and writing assessments is finished and in place, it is simpler to align grading practices and reporting systems at this point. Administrators can announce the transition to teachers at the first staff meeting of the year and to parents through the school's newsletter, in an email, or at a back-to-school night. Although a firm foundation has been laid, administrators should still work to ensure that the message is clear, coherent, and focused on how standards-based grading will move a school or district toward more authentic teaching and learning.

Implement New Report Cards

Thoughtful design of standards-based report cards is an important part of year three. The first step in implementing new report cards is to design and pilot a prototype of the new report card in a few schools or at a few grade levels to identify issues that need to be addressed before schoolwide or districtwide adoption. To begin, consider which grade levels will pilot the new report cards. Often, it is best to transition to new report cards in phases (for example, elementary schools first, then middle schools, then high schools). Next, convene a group of teachers, leaders, and technology support staff to design the content and format of the new report card. The group should examine existing report cards to identify which elements are compatible with standards-based grading and which are not. The group can also discuss the clarity and effectiveness of specific components and adjust them if needed. This process should involve many opportunities for all stakeholders (administrators, teachers, students, and parents) to provide input and feedback about drafts of the report card. Finally, the new report card should be piloted in a few schools or grade levels and revised based on feedback from all stakeholders involved in the pilot. Once a final version of the new report card has been agreed on, it can be implemented school- or districtwide. All stakeholders should understand how the change will affect them (for example, teachers need to know how to grade students and compute their summative scores, and parents need to know how to read the new report cards) and have opportunities to give feedback about the new report cards.

Encourage Small-Group Experimentation

As teachers begin to feel comfortable with the principles of standards-based grading, encourage them—even those not in the guiding team—to experiment with small changes to improve their grading practices before the official implementation. For example, a teacher team might plan to use proficiency scales to assign grades to students during the first semester. Another team might decide to stop using zeros and implement a plan that allows students to retake assessments. These teachers who try new practices and report back about their experiences can help leaders recognize potential issues and work with teachers to solve them. Although these changes are small, they are an important step toward creating teacher-led change.

Organize Book Studies

Book studies keep teachers and administrators informed about recent research and relevant information regarding standards-based grading. They also create a forum in which teachers can share concerns, questions, or lessons learned as they experiment with standards-based grading. To conduct a book study, select a book (or a group of resources), divide up the reading into sections, and discuss one section during each meeting. Leaders could group participants by grade level, department, or collaborative team. Book studies can be voluntary or mandatory. They are especially effective when coupled with professional development workshops or conferences about standards-based grading. The following story illustrates how one district used book studies to support its transition to standards-based grading.

Missy Mayfield found that book studies facilitated her district's transition to standards-based grading. She explained, "Opportunities to dialogue and collaborate on planning, read articles and books, see videos, and have online communication with other teachers who have lived through transitioning from traditional grading to standards-based grading were invaluable experiences for teachers."

One caution for leaders as they implement book studies and other learning opportunities for staff: be sure you closely monitor the pulse of your organization during this time. Moving too fast may make some teachers feel threatened, and they may respond defensively. Focusing on teacher learning (without action) for too long, however, may stall implementation efforts.

Conduct School Visits

Visiting schools where standards-based grading is a reality can give leaders and teachers a clear vision of what is in store for them and their students as they implement standards-based grading. It also provides an opportunity to foresee challenges that other schools have faced and proactively plan to avoid them. The following story illustrates one administrator's approach and reaction to visiting schools already using standards-based grading.

While working on the implementation of standards-based grading for Monroe County Community School Corporation in Bloomington, Indiana, Cameron Rains, then the director of elementary education, took his district's guiding team and scouts to spend a day visiting two schools and one district where standards-based grading was being implemented. They met with teams from each school and observed classrooms. Cameron said, "We obtained very useful information that we were able to take back to our district. Just seeing others working through standards-based grading was so helpful in our implementation efforts."

Start the visiting process by finding the names of schools in your area that have implemented or are in the process of implementing standards-based grading. This is where an outside consultant can be a valuable resource. It is helpful to see a system just slightly ahead of where you are, as it provides insight about next steps to take and potential pitfalls to avoid.

Establish Core Beliefs

One of the tasks addressed by the guiding team is establishing a set of core beliefs about grading, such as the following:

- Reassessment opportunities are important for all students.
- Assigning zeros for missing or incomplete work is not an effective grading practice.

- Grades will be based on proficiency scales connected to prioritized standards.

- Increased grading consistency schoolwide is important.

Establishing core beliefs builds on previous work from year two to uncover current beliefs and attitudes about grading. The members of the guiding team should take current beliefs and attitudes, as well as what they have learned about standards-based grading, into consideration when formulating core beliefs about grading during year three. One way to do this is to have the guiding team members each create an independent list of up to four core beliefs about standards-based grading. After doing so, each member should share his or her beliefs, and then the group should categorize the individual beliefs comma into related groups. If anonymity is important, skip sharing and have each person write each of his or her beliefs on a sticky note. Then use an affinity diagram (see figure 2.1, page 24) to group like beliefs together. Use each category to create an overarching belief statement from the individual beliefs listed there. If you end up with too many belief statements, give each guiding team member three colored sticky dots and ask all of them to place their dots on the beliefs they feel are most important. A member may use all dots on one belief or may spread them out among different belief statements. Review the charts for the belief statements that have the most dots next to them, and use those to create a final standards-based grading core beliefs document.

After the guiding team establishes the core beliefs, ask it to share them with staff. Core beliefs can provide the basis for additional experimentation with standards-based practices by more teachers. They also allow teachers to hold each other accountable to specific, standards-based grading practices. For example, an exasperated teacher might say, "I don't have time to test the first time, let alone allow for retakes." Her teammates can use the core beliefs to encourage and support her as she gets used to new practices. Core beliefs should also be shared with students and parents.

Involve Parents

While some parents may have been involved in various standards-based grading groups and activities during years one and two, year three is an excellent time to communicate with all parents about changes that will be taking place. School leaders should use all of the available formats for parent communication: websites, newsletters, conferences, open houses, service clubs, and parent-teacher organization or association meetings. We also recommend training teachers and staff members to explain changes to parents. School leaders can create lists of important details about standards-based grading that teachers can use while talking to parents and students. This approach helps ensure a consistent message to and from everyone affected by the change. The elevator speech might also be a common communication resource. The following story explains how one of the authors influenced specific parents in his school to communicate with all parents about standards-based grading.

Phil Warrick, former principal at Round Rock High School in Round Rock, Texas, leveraged the connectors within his existing school parent groups to communicate with the larger parent group. He began by discussing grading with his School Parent Advisory Committee. They discussed times when students and parents had felt that grades were unfair and noted that grading was a teaching practice the school was working to improve. Virtually all parents could remember a time when they got an easy A, and others shared concerns about teachers awarding bonus points—often for irrelevant work. Phil shared the history of grading, explaining that many grading practices are similar to those used 150 years ago. He then explained how the high school staff wanted to correct the situation through the implementation of standards-based grading and asked each member to bring a friend to the next meeting, where he repeated the key components of standards-based grading and added some new information and details.

This is an example of one of the many ways that leaders can involve parents and begin helping them think through the concept of grading as it relates to learning. This is also a key opportunity for members of the guiding team to personally interact with parents as partners in changing grading practices.

Involve Technology Staff

A common hurdle for districts and schools implementing standards-based grading is shifting their electronic grading systems to include and reflect prioritized standards, proficiency scales, common assessments, and meaningful grades. While computerized grading programs and electronic gradebooks can be useful tools, they do not relieve teachers of the professional responsibilities involved in making these crucial decisions. In the end, teachers must decide which grade offers the fairest and most accurate description of each student's achievement and level of performance (Guskey & Bailey, 2001).

To help align electronic grading systems with a standards-based approach, a technology expert should be included on the guiding team. When technology experts understand the concept of standards-based grading firsthand, they are better equipped to guide the school's decisions about technology to support it. Often, making technology work for standards-based grading simply requires an individual who understands the benefits of standards-based grading and is willing to make the technology work in ways that support the new system. Conversely, technology staff members who do not understand standards-based grading can be detrimental to the implementation process.

The following story explains how the district technology director for a Colorado Springs, Colorado, school district made existing technology adaptive for the new grading system.

In Michael Storrar's school district, the technology director was able to modify the district's gradebook system so that grades were entered by standard rather than by assignment. He knew that the program had options that could be employed to better connect to standards-based grading needs. This adaptation allowed secondary teachers to connect one assignment to multiple prioritized standards. Teachers could then easily track how students were progressing through the standards rather than simply viewing individual quiz or homework grades. The district's technology staff also created sections in the gradebook to accommodate separate grades for life skills and behavioral factors. Finally, the gradebook was adapted so that teachers could consider a student's pattern of scores when assigning grades rather than using default averaging or central tendency functions.

In the unfortunate event that technology staff do not understand or are unable to modify electronic gradebooks and reporting systems, administrators should feel comfortable contacting technology vendors directly to discuss what options are available to meet a school or district's standards-based grading needs. The following story explains how an administrator who was having trouble with technology adaptations contacted vendors directly for assistance.

To facilitate standards-based grading at Monroe County Community School Corporation in Bloomington, Indiana, Cameron Rains called the district's student data systems company and explained what the district needed the program to do in order to change to a standards-based report card. Within two weeks, the company had adjusted the program to do exactly what he had asked. The district was able to show the growth progress it wanted and still maintain the data and grading systems that teachers had been trained in.

Year Four: Continuation

The important leadership component for year four is ensuring that each element of standards-based grading is strong and continues to be effectively implemented over time. Communication must continue to various constituents such as the board of education, parents, community members, teachers, and students. As teachers become familiar with standards-based grading and try new strategies, they may need forums to talk about their victories, challenges, and lessons learned. Perhaps the most important component of year four is to implement a training and development program for teachers who are new to the school or district.

Implement New-Teacher Development

Standards-based grading will need to be a key development focus each year for teachers who are new to the school or district. Many new teachers are not familiar with standards-based grading, and the guiding team should develop a protocol for training them that addresses three key elements. First, each school should conduct a whole-group introduction to standards-based grading for all new teachers before the start of the school year. Following the whole-group session, new teachers should be given a reflective assessment to determine their level of understanding and where they still have questions. Second, each new teacher should be assigned a mentor teacher for one-on-one tutoring in standards-based grading. Mentor teachers should review new teachers' reflective assessments with them and address specific questions using examples from their own experience. Third, collaborative teams can support new teachers with previously embedded practices such as a common grading policy for the team and previously created common assessments.

Summary

Many leadership qualities and specific strategies help make the change to standards-based grading a success. In this chapter, we outlined the importance of a long-term plan and presented a four-year sample plan that can help leaders think through important components of implementation. We also reviewed suggested considerations for each year and detailed what each of those may entail. Carefully considering how quickly or slowly your staff may need to move will be important as you work through this transformational change. For many leaders, this is the most transformational initiative they lead. To truly make a difference for students in the future, we must review and revise the grading issues of the past.

Epilogue

Transitioning to standards-based grading is a systemic change and must be handled strategically and collaboratively within a school or district. To be successful, school leaders must cultivate collaborative cultures and productive structures necessary to move the initiative forward. Teachers need time to process with one another, try new ideas, receive feedback from peers, and—over time—change existing philosophies. A culture of support, trust, and modeling is important.

Standards-based grading is a particularly salient topic for schools who are interested in becoming high reliability organizations. High reliability organizations are those that "take a variety of extraordinary steps in pursuit of error-free performance" (Weick, Sutcliffe, & Obstfeld, 1999, p. 33). Robert Marzano, Phil Warrick, and Julia Simms (2014) suggested that schools could become high reliability organizations and detailed five levels that schools need to work on to make the transition (as shown in table E.1).

Table E.1: Levels of Operation for a High Reliability School

Level 5	Competency-based education
Level 4	Standards-referenced reporting
Level 3	Guaranteed and viable curriculum
Level 2	Effective teaching in every classroom
Level 1	Safe and collaborative culture

Levels 3, 4, and 5 of the model specifically address grading. The practices, strategies, and guidelines in this book are foundational to making the shifts required by those levels. Chapters 2 and 3 addressed the *guaranteed and viable curriculum* of level 3, chapters 4 and 5 addressed the *standards-referenced reporting* systems of level 4, and chapters 4 and 6 addressed how administrators can guide their schools toward the type of *competency-based education* system that is the focus of level 5, where students matriculate based on their knowledge of the content, rather than time spent in class. Administrators who commit to standards-based grading have the power to propel their schools to the highest levels of reliability and effectiveness. Addressing the issue of grading not only moves schools into a more highly reliable system, but also tackles some of the most concerning inconsistencies in our current systems.

References and Resources

Ainsworth, L. (2003). *Power standards: Identifying the standards that matter the most.* Denver, CO: Advanced Learning Press.

Anderson, L. W., & Krathwohl, D. R. (Eds.). (2001). *A taxonomy for learning, teaching, and assessing: A revision of Bloom's Taxonomy of Educational Objectives* (Complete ed.). New York: Longman.

Barber, M., & Mourshed, M. (2007). *How the world's best-performing school systems come out on top.* New York: McKinsey. Accessed at http://mckinseyonsociety.com /downloads/reports/Education/Worlds_School_Systems_Final.pdf on October 15, 2013.

Black, P., & Wiliam, D. (1998). Assessment and classroom learning. *Assessment in Education: Principles, Policy and Practice, 5*(1), 7–74.

Brookhart, S. M. (2004). *Grading.* Upper Saddle River, NJ: Pearson.

Brookhart, S. M. (2011). Starting the conversation about grading. *Educational Leadership, 69*(3), 10–14.

Brookhart, S. M., & Nitko, A. J. (2008). *Assessment and grading in classrooms.* Upper Saddle River, NJ: Pearson Merrill Prentice Hall.

Burkburnett Independent School District. (2012a). *Burkburnett ISD standards-based grading and assessment 4-year implementation plan.* Unpublished document.

Burkburnett Independent School District. (2012b). *Standards-based grading and assessment focus activities for Burkburnett School District.* Unpublished document.

Campbell, P., Wang, A., & Algozzine, B. (2010). *55 tactics for implementing RTI in inclusive settings.* Thousand Oaks, CA: Corwin Press.

Canady, R. L., & Hotchkiss, P. R. (1989). It's a good score! Just a bad grade. *Phi Delta Kappan, 71*(1), 68–71.

Charantimath, P. M. (2006). *Total quality management.* Singapore: Pearson Education.

Cizek, G. J., Fitzgerald, S. M., & Rachor, R. A. (1995). Teachers' assessment practices: Preparation, isolation, and the kitchen sink. *Educational Assessment, 3*(2), 159–179.

Conley, D. (2000, April). *Who is proficient: The relationship between proficiency scores and grades.* Paper presented at the annual meeting of the American Educational Research Association, New Orleans, LA.

Darling-Hammond, L. (2010). *The flat world and education: How America's commitment to equity will determine our future.* New York: Teachers College Press.

Daro, P., Mosher, F. A., & Corcoran, T. (2011). *Learning trajectories in mathematics* (Research Report #RR-68). Philadelphia: Consortium for Policy Research in Education.

Douglas County School District. (2003). *Reporting form for nonacademic factors.* Unpublished document.

Douglas County School District. (2007). *Proficiency scale for life science: Structure and function.* Unpublished document.

DuFour, R., & Marzano, R. J. (2011). *Leaders of learning: How district, school, and classroom leaders improve student achievement.* Bloomington, IN: Solution Tree Press.

Educational Testing Service. (2003). *Linking classroom assessment with student learning.* Accessed at www.ets.org/Media/Tests/TOEFL_Institutional_Testing_Program /ELLM2002.pdf on October 30, 2013.

Fisher, D., & Kopenski, D. (2008). Using item analyses and instructional conversations to improve mathematics achievement. *Teaching Children Mathematics, 14*(5), 278–282.

Fleenor, A., Lamb, S., Anton, J., Stinson, T., & Donen, T. (2011). The grades game. *Principal Leadership, 11*(6), 48–52. Accessed at www.nassp.org/Content/158/pl_feb11 _fleenor.pdf on October 23, 2013.

Friedman, S. J., & Frisbie, D. A. (2000). Making report cards measure up. *Education Digest, 65*(5), 45–50.

Fullan, M. (2008). *The six secrets of change: What the best leaders do to help their organizations survive and thrive.* San Francisco: Jossey-Bass.

Gandal, M., & Vranek, J. (2001). Standards: Here today, here tomorrow. *Educational Leadership, 59*(1), 6–13.

Gladwell, M. (2000). *The tipping point: How little things can make a big difference.* Boston: Little, Brown.

Guskey, T. R. (2001). Helping standards make the grade. *Educational Leadership, 59*(1), 20–27.

Guskey, T. R. (2002). Computerized gradebooks and the myth of objectivity. *Phi Delta Kappan, 83*(10), 775–780.

Guskey, T. R. (2006). Making high school grades meaningful. *Phi Delta Kappan, 87*(9), 670–675.

Guskey, T. R. (2009a, April). *Bound by tradition: Teachers' views of crucial grading and reporting issues*. Paper presented at the annual meeting of the American Educational Research Association, San Francisco, CA.

Guskey, T. R. (Ed.). (2009b). *The principal as assessment leader*. Bloomington, IN: Solution Tree Press.

Guskey, T. R. (Ed.). (2009c). *The teacher as assessment leader*. Bloomington, IN: Solution Tree Press.

Guskey, T. R. (2011). Five obstacles to grading reform. *Educational Leadership, 69*(3), 16–21.

Guskey, T. R., & Bailey, J. M. (2001). *Developing grading and reporting systems for student learning*. Thousand Oaks, CA: Corwin Press.

Guskey, T. R., Swan, G. M., & Jung, L. A. (2011). Grades that mean something: Kentucky develops standards-based report cards. *Phi Delta Kappan, 93*(2), 52–57.

Hamilton, L., Halverson, R., Jackson, S. S., Mandinach, E., Supovitz, J. A., & Wayman, J. C. (2009). *Using student achievement data to support instructional decision making* (NCEE 2009–4067). Washington, DC: National Center for Education Evaluation and Regional Assistance, Institute of Education Sciences, U.S. Department of Education. Accessed at http://ies.ed.gov/ncee/wwc/pdf/practice_guides/dddm_pg _092909.pdf on October 23, 2013.

Hattie, J., & Timperley, H. (2007). The power of feedback. *Review of Educational Research, 77*(1), 81–112.

Heflebower, T. (2009). Proficiency: More than a grade. In T. R. Guskey (Ed.), *The teacher as assessment leader* (pp. 111–133). Bloomington, IN: Solution Tree Press.

Heritage, M. (2008). *Learning progressions: Supporting instruction and formative assessment*. Washington, DC: Council of Chief State School Officers.

Hoerr, T. R. (2007). What is instructional leadership? *Educational Leadership, 65*(4), 84–85.

Hughes, C. A., & Dexter, D. D. (2011). Response to intervention: A research-based summary. *Theory Into Practice, 50*(1), 4–11.

Individuals with Disabilities Education Improvement Act of 2004. 20 U.S.C. §1400 (2006). Accessed at http://idea.ed.gov/explore/view/p/%2Croot%2Cstatute%2CI%2 CA%2C602%2C3%2CA%2C on March 4, 2014.

Jung, L. A., & Guskey, T. R. (2010). Grading exceptional learners. *Educational Leadership, 67*(5), 31–35.

Kagan, S., & Kagan, M. (2009). *Kagan cooperative learning*. San Clemente, CA: Kagan.

Kanold, T., & Ebert, J. (2010). 1 district, 1 set of math goals. *Journal of Staff Development, 31*(5), 12–14.

Kirk, S., Gallagher, J., Coleman, M. R., & Anastasiow, N. (2012). *Educating exceptional children* (13th ed.). Belmont, CA: Cengage.

Knoebel, M. (2012). *Proficiency scale for physical education: Aerobic exercise.* Unpublished document.

Kotter, J., & Rathgeber, H. (2005). *Our iceberg is melting: Changing and succeeding under any conditions.* New York: St. Martin's Press.

Lake Washington School District. (2010). *Proficiency scale for earth science: Landforms.* Unpublished document.

Lewis, A. C. (1996). Making sense of assessment. *The School Administrator, 53*(11), 8–12.

Locke, E. A., & Latham, G. P. (1990). *A theory of goal setting and task performance.* Englewood Cliffs, NJ: Prentice Hall.

Lomax, R. G. (1996). On becoming assessment literate: An initial look at preservice teachers' beliefs and practices. *Teacher Educator, 31*(4), 292–303.

Marzano, R. J. (2000). *Transforming classroom grading.* Alexandria, VA: Association for Supervision and Curriculum Development.

Marzano, R. J. (2006). *Classroom assessment and grading that work.* Alexandria, VA: Association for Supervision and Curriculum Development.

Marzano, R, J. (2007). *The art and science of teaching: A comprehensive framework for effective instruction.* Alexandria, VA: Association for Supervision and Curriculum Development.

Marzano, R. J. (2009). *Designing & teaching learning goals & objectives.* Bloomington, IN: Marzano Research.

Marzano, R. J. (2010). *Formative assessment & standards-based grading.* Bloomington, IN: Marzano Research.

Marzano, R. J., & Kendall, J. S. (2007). *The new taxonomy of educational objectives* (2nd ed.). Thousand Oaks, CA: Corwin Press.

Marzano, R. J., & Pickering, D. J. (with Heflebower, T.). (2011). *The highly engaged classroom.* Bloomington, IN: Marzano Research.

Marzano, R. J., Pickering, D., & Pollock, J. (2001). *Classroom instruction that works: Research-based strategies for increasing student achievement.* Alexandria, VA: Association for Supervision and Curriculum Development.

Marzano, R. J., Warrick, P., & Simms, J. A. (with Livingston, D., Livingston, P., Pleis, F., Heflebower, T., Hoegh, J. K., & Magaña, S.). (2014). *A handbook for high reliability schools: The next step in school reform.* Bloomington, IN: Marzano Research.

McKnight, J. (1995). *The careless society: Community and its counterfeits.* New York: Basic Books.

McMillan, J. H., Myran, S., & Workman, D. (2002). Elementary teachers' classroom assessment and grading practices. *Journal of Educational Research, 95*(4), 203–213.

McTighe, J., & Ferrara, S. (2000). *Assessing learning in the classroom.* Washington, DC: National Education Association.

McTighe, J., & O'Connor, K. (2005). Seven practices for effective learning. *Educational Leadership, 63*(3), 10–17.

Mellard, D. F., & Johnson, E. S. (2008). *RTI: A practitioner's guide to implementing response to intervention.* Thousand Oaks, CA: Corwin Press.

Missouri Department of Elementary and Secondary Education. (2013). *Missouri comprehensive data system: Achievement level 4 chart—public.* Accessed at http://mcds .dese.mo.gov/guidedinquiry/Achievement%20Level%20%204%20Levels /Achievement%20Level%204%20Chart%20-%20Public.aspx on October 30, 2013.

National Governors Association Center for Best Practices & Council of Chief State School Officers. (2010a). *Common Core State Standards for English language arts and literacy in history/social science, science, & technical subjects.* Washington, DC: Authors. Accessed at www.corestandards.org/wp-content/uploads/ELA_Standards .pdf on March 28, 2014.

National Governors Association Center for Best Practices & Council of Chief State School Officers. (2010b). *Common Core State Standards for mathematics.* Washington, DC: Authors. Accessed at www.corestandards.org/wp-content/uploads/Math_Standards.pdf on March 28, 2014.

No Child Left Behind (NCLB) Act, Pub. L. No. 107–110, § 115, Stat. 1425 (2002).

O'Connor, K. (2007). *A repair kit for grading: 15 fixes for broken grades.* Portland, OR: Educational Testing Service.

Olson, L. (1995, June 14). Cards on the table. *Education Week,* 23–28.

Ornstein, A. C. (1995). *Teaching: Theory into practice.* Boston: Allyn and Bacon.

Popham, W. J. (2003). *Test better, teach better: The instructional role of assessment.* Alexandria, VA: Association for Supervision and Curriculum Development.

Postman, N. (1994). *The disappearance of childhood.* New York: Vintage Books.

Reeves, D. B. (2006). *The learning leader: How to focus school improvement for better results.* Alexandria, VA: Association for Supervision and Curriculum Development.

Reeves, D. B. (2008). Leading to change: Effective grading practices. *Educational Leadership, 65*(5), 85–87.

Reeves, D. B. (2011). Taking the grading conversation public. *Educational Leadership, 69*(3), 76–79.

Rooney, J. (2008). The principal connection: Taking hold of learning. *Educational Leadership, 66*(3), 82–83.

Roschewski, P. K. (2002). *Promising practices, processes, and leadership strategies: Building quality local assessment* (Doctoral dissertation). Accessed at ETD collection for University of Nebraska-Lincoln. (Paper No. AAI3074097)

Ruiz-Primo, M. A., & Furtak, E. M. (2007). Exploring teachers' informal formative assessment practices and students' understanding in the context of scientific inquiry. *Journal of Research in Science Teaching, 44*(1), 57–84.

Scriffiny, P. L. (2008). Seven reasons for standards-based grading. *Educational Leadership, 66*(2), 70–74.

Skillings, M., & Ferrell, R. (2000). Student-generated rubrics: Bringing students into the assessment process. *The Reading Teacher, 53*(6), 452–455.

Stiggins, R. J. (1991). Facing the challenges of a new era of educational assessment. *Applied Measurement in Education, 4*(4), 263–273.

Stiggins, R. J. (2002). Assessment crisis: The absence of assessment *for* learning. *Phi Delta Kappan, 83*(10), 758–765.

Stiggins, R. J. (2008). *An introduction to student-involved assessment for learning* (5th ed.). Upper Saddle River, NJ: Pearson.

Supovitz, J., & Christman, J. B. (2003). *Developing communities of instructional practice: Lessons from Cincinnati and Philadelphia* (CPRE Policy Briefs, RB-39). Philadelphia: UPENN.

Weick, K., Sutcliffe, M., & Obstfeld, D. (1999). Organizing for high reliability: Processes of collective mindfulness. In R. S. Sutton & B. M. Staw (Eds.), *Research in organizational behavior* (vol. 1, pp. 81–123). Greenwich, CT: JAI Press.

Wiggins, G. P. (1993). *Assessing student performance: Exploring the purpose and limits of testing.* San Francisco: Jossey-Bass.

Wiggins, G. P. (1996). Honesty and fairness: Toward better grading and reporting. In T. R. Guskey (Ed.), *ASCD yearbook, 1996: Communicating student learning* (pp. 141–177). Alexandria, VA: Association for Supervision and Curriculum Development.

Wiggins, G., & McTighe, J. (2007). *Schooling by design: Mission, action, and achievement.* Alexandria, VA: Association for Supervision and Curriculum Development.

Winger, T. (2005). Grading to communicate. *Educational Leadership, 63*(3), 61–65.

Winger, T. (2009). Grading what matters. *Educational Leadership, 67*(3), 73–75.

Wolf, K. P. (1993). From informal to informed assessment: Recognizing the role of the classroom teacher. *Journal of Reading, 36*(7), 518–523.

Wormeli, R. (2006). Accountability: Teaching through assessment and feedback, not grading. *American Secondary Education, 34*(3), 14–27.

Index

Effectively track student progress

Signature PD Service

Standards-Based Grading for School and District Leaders Workshop

Transform your school's grading system into one that really shows what students know.

Your team will explore specific aspects of standards-based grading implementation, from identifying prioritized standards and composing proficiency scales to creating aligned assessments and revising report cards. Learn practical steps and strategies for guiding educators, students, and parents through the implementation process, and become acquainted with opportunities and challenges that may arise during the transition.

- Explore concrete steps for implementing standards-based grading.

- Learn to recruit and build teams of educators to prioritize standards and write proficiency scales.

- Discover three kinds of assessments, and learn how to use each type as an effective part of a standards-based grading system.

- Understand the unique grading challenges posed by exceptional learners and how to incorporate accommodations and modifications into grading practices.

- Create an action plan for revising report cards to more clearly communicate student progress and achievement.

Get started!

marzanoreserach.com/OnsitePD
888.849.0851